Islam
Legacy of the Past, Challenge of the Future

Islam

Legacy of the Past,
Challenge of the Future

by
Don Peretz
Richard U. Moench
&
Safia K. Mohsen

NORTH RIVER PRESS

Co-published with
HORIZON/New Horizon Press Publishers

Library of Congress Cataloging in Publication Data

Peretz, Don, 1922-
    Islam : legacy of the past, challenge of the future.

    Bibliography : p.
    1. Islam—20th century. I. Mohsen, Safia K.,
1939-   joint author. II. Moench, Richard U.,
1927-   joint author. III. Title.
BP163.P42   297'.1978   80-27443
ISBN 0-88427-048-3

Contents

Islamic Revival or Reaffirmation, *by Don Peretz*   1

Introduction   1

Origins of Islam   6

Islamic Law and Government   15

Why an Islamic State?   19

Constitutional Principles   25

Islamic Democracy   29

Social Justice   32

The Role of Non-Muslims   36

Women   37

International Relations   39

Islam and Development in Muslim Countries,
by Richard U. Moench   49

Introduction: Obstacles to Understanding   49

Islam and Capitalism   56

Commercial Law and the Sharia   63

Islam and Socialism   66

"None of the Above"   82

Islam and Modern Education   94

Islam: The Legal Dimension, *by Safia K. Mohsen*   99

The Historic Context of Islamic Legislation   100

Crime and Punishment in Islam: Criminal Law   103

Islamic Law and the Family   118

Notes   129

Islamic Revival or Reaffirmation

by

Don Peretz

Introduction

Following the Iranian revolution in 1979, the American news media were saturated with accounts of a worldwide "Islamic revival" and discussions of "the rise of Islam," or "Islam inflamed," in the forty or more countries with a predominantly Muslim population. Cover stories appeared in *Time* and *Newsweek* describing the phenomenon and most of our leading intellectual journals gave space to analysis of the "new" developments.

Americans were so surprised by these events that they became a focal point in discussion of our foreign and national security policies. An impression was created that the Islamic upsurge in the "arc of crisis" stretching from Morocco across North Africa, through the Middle East and South Asia to the Pacific, threatened Western security and jeopardized American interests.

Much of the rhetoric which emanated from Iran's revolutionary council, and the new regime's announced plans to institute an Islamic constitution and government, strengthened Western perceptions of an Islamic revival. Manifestations of growing interest among Muslims in their historic and religious roots are indeed evident, and there can be little doubt that events in Iran since 1979 have been watched closely in the rest of the Muslim world. But this should hardly surprise anyone who has been following political and social developments, or recent trends of thought, in the Muslim world. Increased introspection and self-analysis among Muslim peoples have been widespread since the end of World War II, and they have been accompanied by increased frustration with Western political, social, and economic institutions, and by disappointment with the apparent inability of these institutions to cope with such complex results of Westernization or modernization as rapid population increase,

1

urbanization and industrialization, declining economic productivity, depressed living standards, and increased poverty.

Long before the revolution in Iran, Muslim students in other countries were expressing discontent with the *status quo* through organized Islamic movements. For more than a decade there has been a sharp increase in the number of women at Egyptian universities who returned to traditional dress codes, wearing garments similar to the *chador* adopted by women in Iran. In Jordan several years ago the government set aside rooms in government offices for employees' noon prayers. In Tunisia, President Bourguiba's efforts to secularize have been acknowledged a failure by his closest advisors. And in Malaya there has been increased tension between the country's Muslims and its large Chinese population. Are these manifestations of an Islamic resurgence, a revival; do they indicate a new trend in the Islamic world; or do they represent an outburst of feeling that was dormant in popular consciousness long before the 1979 events in Iran?

Many veteran scholars of the Islamic world were not at all surprised by these events. Some perceive such incidents as "the more or less normal conduct of people who are deeply religious, and who are leading a life founded upon a religious world vision." What many Westerners, including most of our policy makers, failed to recognize was that Islam has been the predominant factor in the daily lives of the world's nearly one billion Muslims for several centuries. The lives of most Muslims have improved little, if at all, since the mid-nineteenth century, despite experiments with Western political and social institutions. To the extent that there was change in the Muslim world resulting from contact with the West, it affected only the small elite at the top of societies in Asia and Africa.

Most Westerners, including our policy makers, have perceived the Muslim world through the eyes of this Western-educated elite; thus we were led to believe that Western-style modernization and secularization progressed much more than it actually did. The impression prevailed that Western ideas and ideologies derived from Marx, or from liberal socialism, or from European democracy, were taking root in the Muslim East. Many of the elite of the Muslim world were themselves convinced that the Islamic roots of their societies would either wither away or be grafted on to new superstructures transplanted from the West. Because most Western contacts with this region have been through its elite—through students in American or

European universities, through diplomats educated in institutions such as Oxford, Harvard, or the Sorbonne, or through businessmen and professionals eager to emulate Western modes, the extent and depth of Islamic consciousness was unknown, or lost sight of.

The modern political and social history of the Muslim world is one of repeated attempts to adopt, to emulate, or to adapt Western-style institutions. Most of the constitutions, the modes of organizing political groups, the methods of mobilizing mass support, and many of the legal systems of the region were borrowed from nineteenth-century Britain, France, Belgium, or Switzerland. From the era of the Ottoman "reform," or Tanzimat, to the Shah's "White Revolution" in the 1960s, the political history of the region is replete with efforts to modernize à la the West. Where, we might ask, have such efforts been successful?

There have been appearances of success. Twentieth-century Turkey, especially since establishment of the Republic by Kemal Ataturk, is a prime example. Egypt between the two World Wars, during the constitutional monarchy, is another. The most recent example was Iran under Shah Mohammed Pahlavi.

So glowing was the image projected of Iran's transition from a traditional to a modern society, that President Carter was, until quite recently, overcome by enthusiasm with events there. During a New Year's Eve celebration on the last night of 1977, Carter toasted the Shah with these words: "Iran, because of the great leadership of the Shah, is an island of stability in one of the more troubled areas of the world. This is a great tribute to you, Your Majesty, and to your leadership, and to the respect and the admiration and love which your people give to you. . . . We have no other nation on earth who is closer to us in planning for our mutual military security. We have no other with whom we have closer consultations on regional problems that concern us both. And there is no leader with whom I have a deeper sense of personal gratitude and personal friendship."[1]

As in Iran, experiments with Western institutions in nearly every country of the Muslim world have always reached a point where they ran into difficulties. In some instances, such as Turkey, there is a slow process of erosion during which Western institutions become less and less useful in dealing with such concrete problems as spiraling inflation, massive unemployment, failure to increase economic productivity, and rapid population increase. When the elite are no longer able to find relevant answers to these problems through Western institutions or ideologies, the masses frequently are led to believe that a return to Islam will bring salvation.

Western political alignments have been as disappointing as Western ideas and ideologies. Most Muslim leaders maintain that the critical tests of relationships with Great Britain, France, or the United States have failed. The belief prevails in Turkey that the United States is on the side of Christian Greece against Muslim Turkey in the Cyprus dispute. In the Arab world the touchstone is the Palestine question. And in Iran thirty years of American support for the "godless" Shah was the crucial test.

True, many of the elite of Muslim countries have maintained close ties with the West. A large number of political leaders were educated in and preserve affiliations with, metropolitan centers such as New York, London, and Paris. Even when political stresses are intense, these ties remain strong. While Egypt's President Nasser was fulminating against the United States during the 1960s, the sons of his foreign minister continued their studies in an American school. And today thousands of Iranians, Turks, Pakistanis, and Arabs receive their higher education in the United States. Although the size of this Western-educated elite is rapidly expanding to tens and hundreds of thousands, it is still an elite, often far removed from the Islamic masses.

Muslim experience with the Communist world has also borne bitter fruit. The success of Marxist ideas and institutions has been even less than that with Western political forms. During the first decades after World War II Marxist affiliations were proscribed in most of the Muslim world. Since the 1960s, when some countries lifted prohibitions on Marxist parties and publications, the ideology failed to take root. Even in most countries where the left found opportunity to enter political contests, it received little if any mass support. In Egypt and Syria during the 1960s, Marxist groups remained elitist associations, unable to rally a large public following. The Turkish Labor Party, the Tudeh in Iran, and the Communist parties in Syria and Iraq were also unable to mobilize mass backing.

Relations with the Soviet Union have been as disappointing as those with the Western powers. Despite propaganda tales during the 1960s and 1970s about Egypt, Syria, and Iraq being absorbed into the Soviet orbit, relations between the USSR and these once so-called "satellites" have degenerated or totally collapsed.

Some secular movements in the Muslim world such as the Wafd party in Egypt, and the Baath parties in Syria and Iraq, attracted many followers. But their influence was short-lived, and they were unable to sustain mass support. On the other hand, groups such as the Muslim Brotherhood in Egypt and the *Shiite* movement in Iran have sustained their influence for half a century or more.

From Morocco to Malaya there is increased disillusionment with experiments in non-Islamic political organization. Recent headline events in Iran, Turkey, Pakistan, Malaya, and other Muslim countries indicate not so much a rebellion against secular authority, as discontent with deteriorating economic and social conditions, expressed in traditional Islamic terms. Islamic dissidence was expressed in terms of a demand for a more equitable social ethic long before the intrusion of Western ideologies. Opposition movements in protest against regimes perceived as arbitrary and tyrannical by the masses were not unique in Muslim society.

Islamic ideas about government, society, and relations of the society with the non-Muslim world are not monolithic. They are nearly as diverse as the social and political ideologies of the West. There are Muslim radicals and conservatives, reformers and traditionalists. But at the heart of all Islamic ideology there is an Islamic core where the diversity of political and social thought originates.

The purpose of this monograph is to examine some prevailing Muslim conceptions of government and society as perceived by Muslims. Although many of these expressions of political and social thought are fairly easy for the average reader to understand, they have been distorted when viewed through the lenses of Western media or seen against a background of riots, demonstrations, and other media events. We have been left with images of "Islamic fanaticism," Muslim "hatred of the West," and other similar stereotypes.

There is much discussion of the Islamic state, the Islamic system of law and justice, an Islamic economic system, and the Islamic law of nations in the Muslim world today. These may be confusing concepts to most Westerners with little or no knowledge of Islam. This book will attempt to explain, from a Muslim perspective, what some of these concepts mean.

Origins of Islam

It is important to understand that in Islam there is no separation of religion and politics, religion and social organization, or religion and law, whether domestic or international. The basis of social organization and law is not a social contract between ruler and ruled, nor among contending groups in society. Islam starts from the fundamental assumption "that all aspects of natural life have been God-willed and possess, therefore, a positive value of their own, the Quran makes it abundantly clear that the ultimate purpose of all creation is the compliance of the created with the will of the Creator. In the case of man, this compliance—called *islam*— is postulated as a conscious, active coordination of man's desires and behavior with the rules of life decreed by the Creator."[2] According to Muhammad Asad, "Islam fulfills this need by means of a Divine Law—called *shari'ah*—which has been provided in the ordinances of the Qur'an and supplemented (or, rather, detailed and exemplified) by the Prophet Muhammad in the body of teachings which we describe as his *Sunna,* or way of life. From the viewpoint of the believer, the Qur'an and the Sunna reveal to us a conceptually understandable segment of God's all-embracing plan of creation. With reference to man, they contain the only available positive indication of what God wants us to be and to do."[3]

"Islam is the community of Allah," writes Gustave E. von Grunebaum in *Medieval Islam.*

> He is the living truth to which it owes its life. He is the center and goal of its spiritual experience. But he is also the mundane head of his community which he not only rules but governs. He is the reason for the state's existence, he is the principle of unity . . . which both upholds and justifies the continuance of the common wealth. This makes the Muslim army the "Army of Allah," the Muslim treasury, "the Treasury of Allah." What is more, it places the life of the community in its entirety as well as the private lives of the individual members under his direct legislative and supervisory power.[4]

Before discussing Islamic concepts of government and law, it would be useful to describe briefly some of the basic ideas of the faith, and to trace its origins. Central to the Islamic faith is its strict monotheism.⁵ God, or *Allah*, is paramount and has no partner. Acceptance of the fundamental doctrine, there is no god but God (Allah), is the rock upon which Islam is founded, the essence of Islam, and the basis upon which Islamic beliefs have developed. The second most important dogma is affirmation that Muhammad is the messenger or apostle of God. He was the last, or the "seal of the prophets." Acceptance of Islam requires only that the believer accept these two dogmas; by uttering the phrase, in Arabic, "there is no god but Allah, and Muhammad is his prophet," one is accepted as a Muslim. This phrase is part of the call to prayer, and the one most repeated in Muslim ritual.

Additional Islamic principles and dogma were recorded in the *Quran* (meaning "recitations") revealed to the Prophet by the Angel Gabriel several times during the latter days of Muhammad's life. Its 114 chapters (*suras*) were collected after Muhammad's death, for there was no written record of them. During his life they were transmitted to his companions and followers orally. By the tenth century there were several versions of the Prophet's recitations. Only then were they amalgamated into the present text of the Quran.

Many of the parables and stories in the Quran are identical or parallel to those in the Old and New Testaments and their associated literatures. There are stories of Adam, Noah, Abraham, Joseph, David, Solomon, Elija, Job, Zachariah, John the Baptist, Mary, and Jesus. Some Quranic descriptions of Judgment Day, the Resurrection, Paradise and Hell, and the angels and devils are presented in vivid language similar to that in Judaic and Christian scripture.

For true believers, the Quran is the final authority on all matters it treats. It provides fundamental guidance for all of life's interrelationships and for its most intimate details. From it has developed the Islamic social system, Islamic law, and Islamic government. It contains a detailed regimen for conduct of the individual, the state, and all of society. Fundamentalist Muslims believe that it contains adequate guidance for all levels of society, thus the slogan of the Muslim Brothers, "the Quran is our constitution."

Pious Muslims believe that the Quran can be transmitted only in its original language, thus Arabic has become a bond of educated Muslims throughout the world. (Not until the 1920s did republican Turkey become the first country to authorize its translation, into modern Turkish.) The Quran is still the basic text for students in mosque schools throughout the Muslim world. It is a style manual and grammar in the study of the Prophet's tongue, Arabic. In Muslim theological colleges it is the basis of the entire curriculum. In Islamic courts it is the root of all jurisprudence.

Religious duties are divided into five categories, called "the pillars of Islam." The first is profession of the *shihada,* the fundamental belief that "there is no god but Allah and Muhammad is his messenger, or prophet." Worship or ritual prayer is the second duty, prescribed five times daily between daybreak and nightfall. The pious Muslim prays wherever he may be, alone if necessary, although group prayer in unison and in a mosque is preferable.

Almsgiving as a manifestation of piety and love is the third pillar. The Prophet initiated the practice with a 2.5 percent levy on the produce and income of his followers for the public treasury. The proceeds were used for the poor, to erect public buildings, and to defray government and other public expenditures. When the Islamic state no longer had the authority to collect the tax, almsgiving became an act of piety.

The fourth pillar is fasting during the Muslim month of *Ramadan.* During Ramadan no food, drink, medicine, or smoke may enter the lips of the pious between dawn and sunset. Bleeding and leech applications, once part of medical procedures, and sexual intercourse are also banned. In some Muslim countries the obligation is legally enforced, with special police to oversee enforcement.

Pilgrimage, the fifth pillar of Islam, is enjoined on all able-bodied Muslims who can afford it, at least once in a lifetime. This institution, called *haj,* was incorporated into Islamic practice by Muhammad from ancient pre-Islamic rites practiced in Arabia. During the Muslim month of haj, members of the faith from all over the world gather in Mecca for worship and to carry out a prescribed ritual at the *Qaaba,* a large ancient building housing a sacred black meteoric rock. Tradition has it that Isaac was to have sacrificed his son Jacob on this site, but was freed from the test at the last moment. During the month of haj pilgrims carry out several exercises and rituals similar to those of pre-Islamic times. Before Islam, the Qaaba was also a sacred site, containing many idols worshiped by pilgrims who had not yet become monotheists. Since Muhammad's death non-Muslims may not enter Mecca. The haj is one of the unifying experiences of Muslims throughout the world, for it brings together followers of all races, nationalities, and ethnic backgrounds in a ritual shared by all. Distinctions of class and national origin are obscured during the ritual, when all participants wear an identical simple white garment and follow the same procedures.

The central figure of Islam is the Prophet Muhammad (Most Highly Praised). While other prophets in the Old and New Testaments are revered and are believed to have carried God's message, Muhammad, "the seal of the prophets," carried divine revelation to its completion and to its perfection. Although some Muslims cite Abraham as "the first Muslim," Muhammad was the historical figure responsible for Islam's emergence as a faith distinct from, although intimately related to, Judaism and Christianity. So esteemed is Muhammad that his name is perhaps the most widely given to Muslim males throughout the world.

Although revered, Muhammad is not worshiped in Islam as is Jesus by many Christians. While the Prophet is considered holy, he was also a man with the foibles, the problems, the disappointments, the appetites and pleasures of other men. In this respect Muhammad seems closer to the actual daily lives of his followers, and more of a realistic historical figure, than Jesus Christ.

The exact date of Muhammad's birth is uncertain (between A.D. 570 and 580). He was the scion of a notable family of Mecca; his grandfather had been a keeper of the Qaaba. When he was about forty years old he received his first revelations from the Angel Gabriel and began to preach in Mecca.

In Mecca he succeeded in winning only a handful of followers to Islam (submission to the will of Allah). His central theme of monotheism was subversive of the *status quo* because it endangered established practices of polytheistic worship at the Qaaba from which Mecca's merchants derived great profits. In 622 Muhammad and his small entourage moved to the town of Medina about 200 miles from Mecca. This *hijra* ("Hejira," migration or exodus) was later designated as the beginning of the Muslim era and marks the first year of the fourteen-century-old Muslim calendar. In Medina his following increased rapidly, and he soon became a central figure of the community. Within a few years he was Medina's leading warrior, legislator, judge, and civil administrator. His experiences and his record as leader of Medina became the model for the classic Muslim state later established in diverse parts of the Islamic world. The Prophet's experience in rulership, in legislation, in relations with non-Muslim minorities, and in international relations during the Medina era became the basis for modern Islamic jurisprudence and international behavior.

Soon after he became the established leader of Medina, Muhammad led his followers back to Mecca. After several battles with the Meccans, the latter also accepted the Prophet and his message. The Qaaba then became the most holy site in Islam. By the time the Prophet died in 632, much of the Arabian peninsula was conquered and Islamic authority was acknowledged by most of its inhabitants. Islam had become not only a religious belief, but a new way to organize the community and to guide society.

Traditionally, community relationships in Arabia had been based on tribal associations derived from blood relationships. Intrafamily blood feuds were common and the cause of continual warfare. Muhammad sought to replace the traditional blood ties with a community of belief which would unite the fighting clans. His extensive use of existing customs and practices such as tribal traditions of treatment for friends and guests, and their absorption into Islamic practice, gave Islam a mass appeal. It did not appear as a foreign import or an esoteric belief of a small elite group. Thus Islam sparked a unity enabling the Arabs of Arabia to overcome divisive local loyalties and to form an effective fighting force which carried the Prophet's message into non-Arab territory far beyond Arabia.

Within a century an Arab-Islamic empire reached from Spain to India—it included all of North Africa, the Levant, and Persia. At first the Arabs did not proselytize Islam beyond the Arabian peninsula; it was considered an Arab faith. Members of other monotheistic religions, including Judaism, Christianity, and Zoroastrianism, were permitted to practice their faiths, although Islam was the state religion and its members were given preferential treatment. The Muslims at first separated themselves from the subject peoples in garrison towns scattered throughout the empire. Gradually Arabic and Islamic influence spread from the garrisons throughout the conquered areas. The regions closest to Arabia became Arabic in language and culture, although many non-Muslims with sophisticated and complex religions remained, retaining their distinctive cultural traits. The Egyptian Copts, the Jews, and various Eastern rite Christian minorities were among these.

In a far more extensive area whole populations converted to Islam without absorbing the Arabic language and culture. The non-Arab Islamic area came to include many times the number of Arabs; it included countries with large populations such as Turkey, Iran, Pakistan, India, Malaya, and Indonesia.

After Muhammad's death and the expansion of the Islamic empire through many cultures and diverse social systems, questions arose that were not answered in the Quran. Guidance was sought in what has become the second most authoritative source after the Quran—the *Hadith* (story, narration, report) or collected traditions of the Prophet. These are sayings or statements attributed to Muhammad by his companions and by later followers. They were compiled in six collections that form the common law of Islam, the *Sunna.* It took about two centuries for Hadith to become accepted as an authentic source of Muslim law. Those who follow the Sunna are called Sunni Muslims, and they are some 90 percent of all Muslim followers today. The other 10 percent are Shiite Muslims, and they are concentrated in Iran. They too have their own collections of Hadith.

The authenticity of the Prophet's sayings, or Hadith, determines the degree of their authority as religious precepts. Authenicity, hence authority, is determined by the reliability of the chain (*isnad*) of transmitters. The most authoritative isnad can be traced back directly to one of the prophet's companions who heard the Hadith in question from Muhammad himself. An example of a chain (isnad) of transmitters would be: A (the last narrator) heard from B, on the authority of C, who said on the authority of D, that the Prophet of God said. . . . Codification of Hadith became a science or discipline a century after Muhammad's death. Out of hundreds of thousands of Hadiths, many were judged to be forged by classical scholars and were not included in the six collections of "authentic" sayings. In some respects the Hadith collections resemble Talmudic commentary of Jewish scholars and rabbis on the Old Testament. They provide guidance in everyday living on nearly all aspects of life for the faithful. In present-day attempts to devise a relevant Islamic constitutional law, Hadith provides extensive authority and support. As we shall see further on, most contemporary discussions of Islamic law and jurisprudence draw heavily from Hadith.

In the expanding and complex Muslim empire, Hadith also became inadequate to meet growing legal needs. Additional rules were devised by jurists who acted initially according to their own concept of right. They often used their own "personal judgment" or "considered personal opinion" (*ray*) based on analogy. This type of jurisprudence was quite free and very subjective, and it thus produced many conflicting religious and legal opinions. An attempt was made to systematize the individual's use of analogy (*qiyas*) by which it was possible to extend a rule in the Quran or Sunna to any local situation. It was felt that if the great jurists acted collectively there would be less chance of error. Thus consensus (*ijma*) of the jurists representing the Islamic community emerged as a later manifestation of God's will.

> Because of its very nature, Ijma' is the most potent factor in expressing and shaping the complex of belief and practice of the Muslims, and at the same time the most elusive one in terms of its formation. It is an organic process. Like an organism it both functions and grows: at any given moment it has supreme functional validity and power and in that sense is 'final' but at the same moment it creates, assimilates, modifies and rejects. That is why its formation could not be vested in any institution. The body of scholars and lawyers that grew rapidly in the first/ seventh and second/eighth centuries and thence onwards could discuss and formulate the results of their thinking which were very influential, especially when they agreed (or rather concurred —this is known as the Ijma' of Scholars), but the formation of Ijma' could not be achieved in the schoolroom. It was more akin to an enlightened public opinion in whose creation the formulation of schools was the most potent factor but which, as we shall see, gradually vetoed many schools of law and theology even out of existence and discredited or modified or expanded the validity of others.[6]

Classic Islamic jurisprudence recognized as the basis of law the Quran, the Sunna recorded in the Hadith, and the consensus (ijma) of the jurists, with analogical deductions (qiyas) if they were based on consensus. Together this body of rules and theological interpretations builds the *Sharia*, or straight path of sacred law. The religious courts that administer it are called Sharia courts. The compilations of legal interpretations cover all aspects of religious, political, civil, and family life, including marriage, divorce, inheritance, and adoption.

Various schools of Islamic thought and legal interpretation arose to cope with the variety of social systems ranging from the French along the Atlantic in Morocco, to the Indian in South Asia. By the tenth century several schools of thought had crystallized, and the right of free interpretation (*ijtihad*) fell into abeyance. The "door of *ijtihad* was closed." Thereafter all Sunni Muslim jurists were obliged to accept the opinions of their predecessors and were deprived of exercising private judgement. While Muslim law and its various schools remained a principal discipline, Islamic theology became moribund, confining itself to the production of commentaries and secondary interpretations—most of which repeated the work of previous scholars.

> Why did this happen? . . . A partial answer is that Islam had passed, during the preceding three centuries, through a period of great conflict of opinions and doctrines and had finally attained stability, through the emergence of an orthodoxy, only toward the end of the third/beginning of the tenth century. When that point was reached and a difficult and stormy formative period had ended, the results were given permanence.[7]

Eventually four Sunni schools survived in Islam, each named for a particular jurist. While differing on fine points, they recognized each other's orthodoxy and often existed side by side in the same areas. Nearly half of Sunnite Islam belongs to the Hanafite school, whose followers predominate in Muslim India and most of the former regions of the Ottoman Empire, now known as the Middle East. The Shafiites prevail in southern Arabia, the East Indies, lower Egypt, Palestine, and East Africa. The more conservative Malikites, who attach importance to the Hadith second only to that of the Quran, are now found in North Africa from Suez to the Atlantic. The most rigid and orthodox school, the Hanbalitites, exist today almost exclusively among the fundamentalist Wahabis of Saudi Arabia.

During the decade of Muhammad's rule and during the period of his first four successors (caliphs), mankind, according to the Muslim theologians, came as close as possible to perfection because of nearness in time to the direct word of Allah. When the Prophet died, Islam was left without a leader, for he had designated no successor. The first caliph was Abu Bakr, Muhammad's father-in-law. He and the next three, Umar (Omar), Uthman, and Ali (the latter being the husband of Fatima, Muhammad's daughter), were called the *Rashidun* (first ones), and were accepted by nearly all Muslims as the Prophet's legal heirs. Ali's succession was disputed by

Muawiya, the governor of Syria, who won the caliphate after Ali's assassination in 661. Muawiya's reign marks the end of the orthodox and idealized era of Islam; it also started the first major schism. Many Muslims refused to accept Muawiya and his heirs as legitimate successors of the prophet. They insisted that the legitimate succession lay with the sons of Ali, Hasan and Husain, who were also killed in the wars of succession. After Husain and most of his followers were massacred at the battle of Karbala in Iraq during 680, those who supported Ali's line became a religious sect and political faction known as Shiites from the Arabic word *Shia* meaning party (the party of Ali). The Shiites absorbed many non-Arab followers, and many Persian customs and traditions, including certain mystical beliefs.

Shiite theologians deprecate Muawiya and his successors as false caliphs, usurpers who follow a false path. Their animosity is intensified by Muawiya's establishment of heredity as the principle of succession to the caliphate, and its transformation into a monarchy with all of the attributes of kingship, including royal palaces, luxurious living, and monarchial absolutism. One of the terms used by the Shiite clergy of Iran to excoriate the recent Shah was that he was the "Yazid (son of Muawiya) of his time."

Shiites attribute special rights to Ali and his successors. They believe that these rights were handed down in a line of *imam*s (religious leaders) with unusual powers. Some Shiites have raised Ali and his sons to as important a place in Islam as the Prophet, and they have endowed the line of Ali with a special mystical aura. The violent deaths of Ali and his sons made them martyrs and bound their followers in a blood pact. Husain's defeat at Karbala is still commemorated annually by a passion play during which the most zealous mourners flagellate themselves until the blood flows in symbolic remembrance of the first martyrs. Most Shiites believe that after Ali and his two sons there were nine more direct, infallible successors, or imams, and that the last of the twelve disappeared in obscure circumstances. Eventually this "hidden" or "expected" imam will reappear as the *Mahdi* (Rightly Guided One), a saviour or messiah of mankind. Until his coming, Islam is to be interpreted by scholars acting as the Mahdi's agents. This predominant Shiite group is known as the *Imami* or "Twelvers," and it is the dominant religious factor in Iran.

Within Islam religious controversy often played the role that politics plays in the modern world; it has been an outlet for economic and social discontent. Within Shiite Islam the Ismailis were such a group. They inherited the revolutionary character of the early Shiite movement and gathered urban and rural disaffected into an offshoot of the Imamis. Factionalization broke out over the succession to the sixth imam. Next in line was Ismail, but the "Twelvers" bypassed him because of his addiction to wine. His followers, the Ismailis, or "Seveners," considered him not only the legal heir but the last or hidden and expected imam for whom the Shiites had been waiting. The contemporary Ismaili leader is the Agha Khan of Pakistan, with followers throughout the Middle East and Africa.

The Zaidis of Yemen left the main branch of Shiism in 731, also in a dispute over succession. They supported Zaid, Ali's great-grandson, in preference to Zaid's brother. Zaid was martyred in an uprising against the Sunni regime in 740. The sect named after him became official in Yemen and is closer to the Sunni community than any other Shiite group.

Other surviving Ismaili offshoots with secret religious rites are the Druzes, now in Syria, Lebanon, Jordan, and Israel, and the Nusayris or Alawis found in northern Syria and in Lebanon. The Alawis became influential in the Syrian Baath party after World War II, and one of their members, Hafez al-Assad, has been the country's leader since 1970.

Islamic Law and Government

During the reign of the Prophet and the first four Rightly Guided caliphs, Islamic society was governed in traditional Arab style. The leader resembled the tribal chieftain who owed his office to personal prestige derived from lineage in a leading family, outstanding qualities of leadership and generosity, and communal consensus. Although Muhammad was an absolute ruler, he received the overwhelming support of the whole community. While the first four caliphs did not have the stature of the Prophet, they too ascended to leadership with extensive support from the community at large. All members of the community had access to the leader, for he was shrouded behind no elaborate ceremonial. On the contrary, Muhammad and his immediate successors established reputations as leaders who lived simple lives unencumbered by extensive property and masses of worldly goods.

As the Muslim domain expanded into an empire and its leaders acquired the aura of royalty, it became increasingly difficult to maintain a rulership style modeled on tribal democracy. Gradually the caliph became as absolute a ruler, one as isolated, as the Roman and Byzantine emperors. Although theory supported the election of both emperor and caliph, practice worked in favor of heredity.

By the tenth century the Muslim empire had fragmented into several separate kingdoms, and the caliphate lost its significance as the center of Islamic political and legal authority. An elaborate civil bureaucracy developed parallel to the religious hierarchy. In each part of the formerly unified Muslim empire, civil administration was strongly influenced by custom and tradition prevailing before the Arab-Muslim conquest.

Von Grunebaum traces five principal strains of culture determining Islamic development. At first Muhammad welded Judeo-Christian with Arabic ideas and values, including much pre-Islamic pagan tradition. Later Hellenic-Greek thought was absorbed through translations from the Syriac. Greek dialectics and methods of allegorical interpretation, and Christian asceticism, were adopted to broaden Islam's base beyond the limitation of the Quran. Discussion of problems according to categories of formal logic, purely theoretical speculation, and a secular science independent of religious sectarianism was Greek in origin. The Persian tradition, itself earlier influenced by Hellenism, shaped the ethics of civic life. Ancient guilds, the Sassanid Persian financial system, and Oriental religious despotism were all present. Indian medicine, pharmacology, mathematics, and possibly Indian mysticism and literary theory also left their imprint on Islamic learning.[8]

Despite the political fragmentation of the Islamic world and spread of the faith to nearly every race or ethnic group, there was a remarkable unity that has remained until the present. The common beliefs and practice of Islam, the magnetic quality of the Quran and the Sunna, and the fact that all Muslim scholars were fluent in Arabic made it possible for a pious member of the faith to be at home anywhere in the wide world of Islam. After division of the empire into several Muslim states, it was not unusual for theologians or scholars to be accepted in the religious establishment of a state other than their own.

After establishment of the Umayyad dynasty in Damascus, officers of the new empire began to interpret Islamic law in the light of local practices in the different provinces. At the same time leaders of the religious community in Medina began to construct principles intended as the basis for a universal Islamic law. The state became the executive institution which applied Sharia law in the various parts of the empire as it was formulated by local legal authorities. Although conventional Muslim jurisprudence (*fiqh*), based on the commands and prohibitions of the Quran and Sunna, was uniform, details differed as the law was influenced by local tradition and custom and by the diverse interpretations of scholars.

When the Abbasid empire declined in the tenth century, the powerful new sultans began to enact their own special laws, and a new body of law developed by the civil authority emerged to supplement the Sharia. Later Muslim layers attempted to integrate the new legislation into the Sharia.

During the era when most of the Middle East, except Iran and central Arabia, was under Ottoman rule, administrators in the Ruling Institution developed a body of regulations parallel to the Sharia called *qanun* (canon), which dealt with matters of government administration, such as taxation, military services, and administrative boundaries. Although the Ottoman sultan also assumed the title of caliph, the qanun law was a product of the sultanate rather than of the caliphate.

While various administrative codes developed throughout the Muslim world, Islamic jurisprudence derived from the Quran and Sunna most affected the average person in daily life. For example, matters of personal status such as marriage, divorce, and inheritance were usually governed by the laws of Islam rather than by the administrative codes. In the Ottoman empire the Religious Institution was parallel to the Ruling Institution, but the average Ottoman subject had greater contact with the religious authorities than with the civil administrators.

Religious law is still administered by the *ulema*, or body of learned men, made up of religious leaders possessing *ilm* (knowledge, especially of Islamic law). A Muslim is considered a member of the ulema after acquiring sufficient formal training in the appropriate religious seminaries. Judges in Islamic courts are selected from the ulema. Specific legal interpretation and its application to individual cases is undertaken by a *Mufti* whose verdict or opinion is called a *fatwa.* Collections of fatwas issued by authoritative ulema over a period of time become the equivalent of collections of case law, and as such, they are used as precedents in the courts. These collections of fatwas provide one of the best sources from which to trace development of Islamic law, for they show how local customary laws were gradually integrated into Islamic law over a long period of time.

As we have seen, the basis of Islamic law, Sharia, is perceived as Divine Law—provided in the ordinances of the Quran and supplemented by the Prophet's teachings, described as his Sunna, or way of life. The whole structure of law rests on the idea of God as sovereign. The purpose of the law, then, is to achieve compliance with God's will. In the case of man, this compliance, called Islam, means coordination of man's desires and behavior with the rules of life decreed by the Creator. Man must be taught to differentiate between good and evil, between the concepts of "right" and "wrong." These concepts have meanings that do not change from case to case or from time to time, but are valid for all times and conditions. "From the viewpoint of the believer, the Quran and the Sunnah reveal to us a conceptually understandable segment of God's all-embracing plan of creation. With reference to man, they contain the only available positive indication of what God wants us to be and to do."[9]

Rather than a specific legal code, Islamic law established the outlines of religious obligations and prohibitions, valid for all time. All human acts are thus divided into five ethical categories: (1) obligatory, (2) recommended, (3) permissible or acts to which God is indifferent, (4) reprehensible, and (5) forbidden.

A tenth-century scholar, Ibn Hazm of Cordova (384-456 Islamic, A.D. 994-1064) described the situation in this way:

> The *shari'ah* in its entirety refers either to obligatory acts [*fard*], the omission of which constitutes a sin; or to forbidden acts [*haram*], the commission of which constitutes a sin; or to allowed acts [*mubah*], the commission or omission of which does not make man a sinner. Now these *mubah* acts are of three kinds: first, acts which have been recommended [*mandub*]—meaning that there is merit in doing them, but no sin in omitting them; second, acts which are undesirable [*makruh*]—meaning that there is merit in abstaining from them, but no sin in committing them;

and, third, acts which have been left unspecified [*mutlaq*]—being neither meritorious nor sinful whether committed or omitted . . .

The Apostle of God said: "Do not ask me about matters which I have left unspoken: for, behold, there were people before you who went to their doom because they put too many questions to their prophets and thereupon disagreed [about their teachings]. Therefore, if I command you anything, do of it as much as you are able to do; and if I forbid you anything, abstain from it."

The above Tradition circumscribes all the principles of religious law [*din*] from the first to the last. It shows that whatever the Prophet has left unspoken—neither ordering nor forbidding it—is allowed [*mubah*], that is, neither forbidden nor obligatory. Whatever he ordered is obligatory [*fard*], and whatever he forbade is unlawful [*haram*]; and whatever he ordered us to do is binding on us to the extent of our ability alone. (Examples of Hadith.)[10]

From this scheme it is obvious that there is a certain freedom of choice in Islam. Believers are left with the possibility of choosing a great many activities that are neither ordered nor forbidden. One is also given freedom of choice—whether or not to behave in the way indicated by God; "and we may, if we choose, go against Him, disregard His law, and risk the consequences. However we decide, the responsibility is ours. It goes without saying that our ability to lead an Islamic life depends on our making the former choice."[11]

Why an Islamic State?

Even if the purpose of the law is to achieve man's righteousness, writes Muhammad Asad, a great deal can become effective only through communal effort. The individual requires the cooperation of the society around him to carry out the law. Social conditions must be created and maintained to enable the greatest number of people to live in harmony, freedom, and dignity. If there is no worldly power responsible for enforcing Islamic law, the community's willingness to carry it out will only be theoretical. Thus, writes Asad: "This responsibility can be discharged only by a coordinating agency invested with the powers of command (*amr*) and prohibition (*nahy*): that is, the state. It follows, therefore, that the organization of an Islamic state or states is an indispensable condition of Islamic life in the true sense of the word."[12]

Muhammad Asad argues against the contemporary association by many intellectuals, both Muslim and non-Muslim, of "secularism" with "progress." Many educated Muslims have been influenced by this Western concept; thus, "instead of submitting their decisions and actions to the criterion of a moral law—which is the ultimate aim of every higher religion—these people have come to regard expediency (in the short-term, practical connotation of the word) as the only obligation to which public affairs should be subjected; and because the ideas as to what is expedient naturally differ in every group, nation, and community, the most bewildering conflicts of interest have come to the fore in the political field, both national and international."[13]

In a modern "secular" state, asserts Asad, the only norm by which to judge between good and evil, and between right and wrong, is the "nation's interest." With no "objective scale of moral values" even within the nation, the result is conflict between widely divergent views of what constitutes the nation's best interest.

It has become evident that none of the contemporary Western political systems—economic liberalism, communism, national socialism, social democracy, and so forth—is able to transform that chaos into something resembling order: simply because none of them has ever made a serious attempt to consider political and social problems in the light of absolute moral principles. Instead, each of these systems bases its conception of right and wrong on nothing but the supposed interests of this or that class or group or nation—in other words, on people's changeable (and, indeed, continuously changing) material preferences. If we were to admit that this is a natural—and therefore desirable—state of man's affairs, we would admit, by implication, that the terms "right" and "wrong" have no real validity of their own but are merely convenient fictions, fashioned exclusively by time and socioeconomic circumstances. In logical pursuance of this thought, one would have no choice but to deny the existence of any moral obligation in human life: for the very concept of moral obligation becomes meaningless if it is not conceived as something absolute. As soon as we become convinced that our views about right and wrong or good and evil are only man-made, changeable products of social convention and environment, we cannot possibly use them as reliable guides to our affairs, and so, in planning those affairs, we gradually learn to dispense with all moral guidance and to rely on expediency alone—which, in turn, leads to ever-growing dissensions within and between human groups and to a progressive decrease in the amount of happiness vouchsafed to man. This is, perhaps, the ultimate explanation of the deep disquiet which is apparent throughout the modern world.[14]

Only religion, argues Asad, can provide the absolute moral law upon which there can be unanimous communal agreement, agreement defining what is right and what is wrong in the affairs of men. This leads to the conclusion that only the Islamic state can provide the required framework for a unified and just community. "Most people of our time have grown accustomed to accepting racial affinities and historical traditions as the only legitimate premises of nationhood: whereas we Muslims, on the other hand, regard an ideological community—a community of people having a definite outlook on life and a definite scale of moral values in common—as the highest form of nationhood to which we can aspire. We make this claim not only because we are convinced that our particular ideology, Islam, is a Law decreed by God Himself, but also because our reason tells us that a community based on ideas held in common is a far more advanced manifestation of human life than a community resulting from race or language or geographical location."[15]

Is the Islamic state envisaged by Muhammad a theocracy as the term is understood in the West? If all temporal legislation flows from what the community considers to be a "Divine Law," the answer is yes. But the answer would be no if one defines theocracy in terms of medieval European history, where a priestly hierarchy was invested with supreme political power. "Since every adult Muslim has the right to perform each and every religious function, no person or group can legitimately claim to possess any special sanctity by virtue of the religious functions entrusted to them. Thus, the term 'theocracy' as commonly understood in the West is entirely meaningless within the Islamic environment."[16]

Some modern Muslims, attempting to apply Western terminology to their environment, assert that Islam is democratic, or even that it seeks the establishment of a socialist society. On the other hand, many Western critics refer to Islamic society as totalitarian, and argue that it must inevitably result in Islamic dictatorship. These terms, writes Asad, are derived from the Western historical experience, and are therefore frequently irrelevant or meaningless in the Islamic context. While they are legitimate and understandable in the Western historical context, they often are wholly out of place within the Islamic world view. Democracy, for example, is used in the sense given it by the French Revolution, namely the principle of socio-economic equality of all citizens, and of government by the entire adult population through its elected representatives, on the basis of "one person, one vote." In this modern context, the "will of the people" appears theoretically as something that is free of all external limitations, sovereign unto itself and responsible only to itself. While Islam, according to Asad, maintains that all human beings are socially equal and must be given the same opportunities for development and self-expression, it is incumbent upon all Muslims

> to subordinate their decisions to the guidance of the Divine Law revealed in the Qur'an and exemplified by the Prophet: an obligation which imposes definite limits on the community's right to legislate and denies to the "will of the people" that attribute of sovereignty which forms so integral a part of the Western concept of democracy. A tendency superficially similar to that of Islam can be discerned in the concept of "ideological" democracy prevalent in the USSR and other Communist states. There, as in Islam, an ideology is placed over and above the people's freedom to legislate for themselves; only within the framework of that ideology can the majority vote become effective. However, as just mentioned, this similarity is only superficial: first, because Islam bases all its ideological concepts on a Divine Law which, to the believer, is ethically binding in an absolute, immutable sense, whereas the ideology of communism is admittedly the product of a human doctrine and is therefore subject to the most far-reaching amendments; and, second, because Islam makes the comprehension and interpretation of its Law dependent on the individual's knowledge and conscience alone and does not force him to accept interpretations by any other individual or organized body as morally binding. (Notwithstanding the frequent violations of this principle in the course of Muslim history, the teachings of Islam are unequivocal on this subject.)[17]

Both liberal and conservative proponents of the Islamic order leave room for flexibility in developing Islamic political forms. Many idealize the early period of the Rashidun under the four Rightly Guided caliphs and designate it as an historical precedent or model for all times. Muhammad Asad, however, maintains that such reliance on historical precedent is an even greater danger than the attempted application of non-Islamic terminology to Islamic political development. Nothing could be more erroneous than the idea that only *one* form of state deserves to be called Islamic. In examining the political ordinances of the Quran and Sunna, he finds that they do not lay down any specific form of state, nor do they elaborate a detailed constitutional theory. Rather, the political law emerging from the Quran and Sunna: ". . . gives us the clear outline of a political scheme capable of realization at all times and under all conditions of human life. But precisely because it was meant to be realized at all times and under all conditions, that scheme has been offered in outline only and not in detail. Man's political, social, and economic needs are time-bound and, therefore, extremely variable. Rigidly fixed enactments and institutions could not possibly do justice to this natural trend toward variation; so the shari'ah does not attempt the impossible. Being a Divine Ordinance, it duly anticipates the fact of historical evolution, and confronts the believer with no more than a very limited number of broad political principles; beyond that, it leaves a vast field of constitution-making activity, of governmental methods, and of day-to-day legislation to the *ijtihad* of the time concerned."[18]

Thus, many forms of the Islamic state are possible. Muslims of each age must discover and form the institutions most suitable to their needs, "on condition, of course, that the form and the institutions they choose are in full agreement with the explicit, unequivocal *shari'ah* laws relating to communal life."

Writings of Hasan al-Banna and other ideologues of the conservative Muslim Brotherhood are also open-ended on the subject of the Islamic state. One of the society's foremost ideologues, Sayyid Qutb, wrote: "When we come to discuss political and economic theory from the practical point of view of the state, we find that the course of history shows an exemplary failure in the life of Islam."[19] Would-be theoreticians "were compelled to emphasize the 'principles' which would guide an Islamic state; the 'specifics' would be left to 'time, place and the needs of the people.' "[20] Some historians suggest that absence of precise guidance on the forms of the Muslim state has resulted from historical indifference to political forms. Muhammad Asad implies that it was divine wisdom that gave man the opportunity to choose and to develop flexible Islamic institutions.

One of the most detailed of the Muslim Brotherhood works on the subject of the Islamic state, by Abd al-Qadir Awda, laid out a number of guidelines. The political structure of the state was to be bound by three fundamental principles: "(1) the Qur'an is the fundamental constitution; (2) government operates on the concept of consultation (*shura*); (3) the executive ruler is bound by the teachings of Islam and the will of the people. Founded on these three principles, the Islamic state would have a just and efficient government, be consistent with the traditions of the society, and be capable of securing the general welfare. The details of organization would follow from these principles."[21]

In answer to fundamentalists who objected to the flexible interpretations of Muhammad Asad, he cited Hadith sanctioning free interpretation. The Hadith tells of a Companion of the Prophet, Muadh, sent as governor to the Yemen. The Prophet asked him: "How will you decide the cases that are brought before you?" Muadh replied: "I shall decide them according to the Book of God." "And if you find nothing concerning [a particular matter] in the Book of God?" "Then I shall decide it according to the Sunna of God's Apostle." "And if you find nothing about it in the Sunna of God's Apostle?" "Then," replied Muadh, "I shall exercise my own judgement . . . without the least hesitation." Thereupon the Prophet slapped him upon the chest and said: "Praised be God, who caused the messenger of God's Messenger to please the latter!"[22]

This Hadith, asserts Asad, demonstrated the Prophet's approval of his Companion's common sense in asserting the right of independent decision on all matters not formulated in terms of law in the Quran and Sunna. None of the Companions, he states, regarded his own ijtihad as binding in a religious sense on any other person. None of them arrogated to himself the status of lawgiver for all times; ". . . all findings obtained through *ijtihad,* by however great a person, are invariably conditioned by that person's environment and state of knowledge: and knowledge, especially in matters of social concern, depends not so much on the loftiness of a man's character as on the sum total of the historical experience available to him."[23]

Constitutional Principles

"It is obvious that our conclusions as to the best means of achieving administrative efficiency and safeguarding social equity are conditioned by the time and the socioeconomic environment in which we live—and so, logically, quite a big proportion of the legislative enactments in an Islamic state must vary from time to time. . . . there can be not the least doubt that an Islamic constitution to be evolved thirteen centuries after the Right-Guided Caliphs may legitimately differ from that which was valid in and for their time."[24]

To illustrate this point, Asad explains that the Sharia is quite clear about the principle of elective government as such. However, the law does not specify any particular method of election, although it is clear that the chief executive of the Islamic state must be elected. Thus each of the four successors of the Prophet was elected, although each of the elections was conducted in a different manner. "Hence, under each of these four reigns which we describe as 'right-guided,' the constitution of the state differed on a most important point. . . . The different treatment accorded by the Companions to this question—with regard to both the composition of the electorate and the electoral procedure—shows that, in their opinion, the constitution of the state could be altered from time to time without making it any the less 'Islamic' on this account."[25]

While the specifics of constitutional arrangements and legislation among Islamic states differ, most of those governed by Islamic law seem to agree on certain principles. Islamic constitutions or state systems based on Islamic law generally place the importance of Islam and unity of the Islamic community over and above that of any individual state or political entity. The new Iranian constitution thus states that: ". . . the government does not arise from the notion of classes and mediation among persons or groups but is a crystallization of political idealism based on religious community and concord which provide it organization—which through the process of ideological transformation turns its path toward the final goal (movement toward God)."[26] As in most other Islamic political systems, the Iranian constitution pays homage to Islamic unity. "According to the Koran, all Muslims are of the same and one single religious community, and the Islamic Republican Government of Iran is bound to base its general policies on the coalition and unity of the Islamic nations, and it should exert continuous efforts in order to realize the political, economic, and cultural unity of the Islamic world.''[27]

Asad also avers that the state is not an end in itself, rather: "The innermost purpose of the Islamic state is to provide a political framework for Muslim unity and cooperation." Proponents of the Islamic state tend to depreciate nationalism of the individual state. It "runs counter to the fundamental Islamic principle of the equality of all men and must, therefore, be emphatically ruled out as a possible basis of Muslim unity," states Asad.[28]

The Muslim Brothers in Egypt also deprecated the Western concept of nationalism, partly because it destroyed Muslim unity, leaving separate Muslim states prey to so-called Christian and Zionist imperialism. ". . . this 'narrow nationalism,' which is a Western product has established 'a new object of worship,' the materialist nation, destructive and incompatible with the 'nationalism of divine principles' decreed by God in Islam. . . . The ultimate and only real relationship possible to men is with God, not with other men; 'there is no higher self-respect . . . than this.' Man, if he is bound primarily by the God-man relationship, and thus free of narrow partisanship and factionalism, is free to unite with other men under the single banner of God. Islam, then, repudiates nationalism narrowly defined by secular and material interests, preferring rather that patriotism serve the larger—and only valid—divinely inspired goals of the community.''[29]

The source of sovereignty in the Islamic political system is not some man-made institution, or even the will of the people, but God. The Iranian constitution thus states: "The absolute ruler of the world and humanity is God and He alone has determined the social destiny of human beings. No one shall take away this God-given right from another person or make use of it to serve his personal or group interests. The nation will use this God-given right to act according to the manner determined by the following principles [outlined in the constitution].''[30]

A draft constitution proposed by a group of Pakistani socialists expresses the same idea under the heading, "Sovereignty of Allah." It states: "The Islamic State of Pakistan is built on the belief that sovereignty belongs to Allah. Everything between the heavens and the earth belongs to Him. This means that all mineral, gas, forest and water resources, as well as undeveloped land being the wealth of Allah, are for the benefit of the Ummah (community). Hence, the

State reserved priority for the development of this portion of the economy."[31]

In most Muslim states, even those not governed by Islamic law, the constitution requires that the leader be Muslim. In states fashioned according to Islamic law, "it is obvious that only a person who believes in the Divine origin of that Law—in a word, a Muslim —may be entrusted with the office of head of the state. Just as there can be no fully Islamic life without an Islamic state, no state can be termed truly Islamic unless it is administered by people who can be supposed to submit willingly to the Divine Law of Islam."[32] While the Muslim Brothers were quite flexible in defining possible models for an Islamic state, they too insisted that the ruler must have certain qualities: "he must be Muslim, male, adult, sane of mind, and healthy in body; he must be knowledgeable in Muslim jurisprudence, just, pious, and virtuous; and he must be capable of leadership."[33] Under the new Iranian constitution, the president, chosen for a four-year term ". . . must be elected from among men of political and religious distinction. He must . . . be pious; be a believer in the foundation of the Islamic Republic of Iran and in the official religion of the country [*Ithna Ashari*—Twelver Shiism]."[34]

Iran's new constitution established a twelve-member Council of Guardians or Leadership Council headed by a religious leader with supreme authority over all branches of government, to assure that all legislation complies with Shiite Islamic principles. The supreme leader, called *Faghi* (trustee or guardian) is to act in place of the twelfth imam of the Shiite sect who disappeared 1,100 years ago, and who, Shiites believe, will return one day. He is called the hidden imam who will return as the Mahdi, similar to the Judeo-Christian concept of messiah. "During the absence of the Glorious Lord of the Age, the twelfth imam of the Shi'ite sect . . . he will be represented in the Islamic Republic of Iran as religious leader and imam of the people by an honest, virtuous, well-informed, courageous, efficient administrator and religious jurist, enjoying the confidence of the majority of the people as a leader."[35]

The Faghi and members of the Leadership Council are required to have: "1. The necessary competence in theology and piety to deliver formal legal opinions and authority . . . [and] 2. enough political and social insight, boldness, strength, and managerial ability to lead."[36] The extensive powers of the Faghi or leader place him above the elected president of the republic and any of the legislative or judicial bodies established by the constitution. The Faghi appoints members of the Council of Guardians and the highest judicial authorities of the country; he commands the armed forces, appointing and dismissing the army chief of staff and commander-in-chief of the Islamic Revolutionary Guards Corps; he has authority to declare war and mobilize the armed forces; he must approve all candidates for the presidency, and formalizes the president's election; he has authority to dismiss the president of the republic, and to pardon or reduce the sentences of convicts, "within the limits of Islamic standards, pursuant to the suggestions of the Supreme Court."[34]

Iran's army, according to the Islamic constitution, ". . . must be an Islamic army. It must be a popular and religiously educated army and it must accept worthy people who will be faithful to the goals of the Islamic Revolution and will be self-sacrificing in the attainment of these goals."[38]

Muhammad Asad argues that a certain amount of "differentiation" between Muslim and non-Muslim is required in the Islamic state, or there would be no possibility of establishing an Islamic state or states in the sense envisaged by the Quran and Sunna. "This does not and cannot mean that we should discriminate against non-Muslim citizens in the ordinary spheres of life. On the contrary, they must be accorded all the freedom and protection which a Muslim citizen can legitimately claim: only they may not be entrusted with the key position of leadership. One cannot escape the fact that no non-Muslim citizen—however great his personal integrity and his loyalty to the state—could, on psychological grounds, ever be supposed to work wholeheartedly for the ideological objectives of Islam; nor in fairness, could such a demand be made of him."[39]

Although the leader is endowed with extensive religious and civil powers in the Islamic state, all Muslim political theoreticians place great emphasis on the principle of consultation. Drawing on the Quran's injunction that members of the community consult among themselves, Muslim Brotherhood theoreticians called "consultation" (shura) a mandatory and fundamental part of the Islamic state. While the Sharia provided general principles, it left room for the community to evolve detailed legislation through consensus achieved in the process of consultation. Since the whole community cannot sit together to legislate, it must delegate its legislative powers to an appropriate body. Some Muslims, using the example of the first four caliphs, assert that temporal legislative powers should be delegated to an all-powerful individual freely elected by the Muslim community. Most Muslim theoreticians, however, citing historical evidence, believe that such an accumulation of power is extremely dangerous. Rather, they advise rule by consultation through a council (assembly, parliament, or other such body).

Islamic Democracy

Muslim Brotherhood theoreticians cite "the nation," or "the people" as the source of all the ruler's power. "The nation alone is the source of power; bowing to its will is a religious obligation." "The ruler has no legal existence and deserves no loyalty except as 'he reflects the spirit of the society and is in harmony with its goals.' " The founder of the Muslim Brotherhood, Hasan al-Banna, called the ruler a "trustee" or "agent" of the Islamic community. Thus, hereditary leadership is not possible in the Islamic state. "The ruler, as the chosen agent of the people, is responsible to them for all his acts—political, civil, or criminal; to his person attaches no special privilege, and if necessary he is subject to trial by ordinary courts. His chief function is the establishment and maintenance of Islam and the execution of its laws, a duty which automatically ensures the general welfare. Obedience derives from the execution of the law—'that is the contract with the ruler'; failure to do so frees the nation from loyalty to him. If he deviates from his assigned tasks, he must be 'warned,' 'guided,' and then removed."[40]

Islamic political theoreticians emphasize the importance of establishing elected councils for the purpose of consultation (shura), based on the Quranic ordinance which called on the Prophet's followers to conduct their communal business by "consultation among themselves." The parliament of the new Iranian Muslim Republic is thus called the National Consultative Assembly and vested with the country's legislative power. The legislative assembly, or *majlis ash-shura,* should therefore represent the whole community. Muhammad Asad states that it should represent both men and women; that its representative character can be achieved only through free general election in which the entire community participates, including men and women. The details of suffrage, states Asad, have not been determined by the Quran or Sunna, and are left to the discretion of the community, "in the light of the requirements of the time."[41]

Based on precedents established by the Prophet, orthodox Muslims are skeptical of those who campaign for office. There are numerous Hadiths citing Muhammad's aversion to those who approached him for such privileges. When he was approached by one of his companions with a request for a post in government, he answered: "By God, we do not appoint to such work any one who asks for it, nor anyone who covets it," (Hadith cited).[42] Other similar Hadiths were: "We consider seekers after posts of trust and responsibility as the most untrustworthy," and "people who are self-seekers or do not serve others are forbidden to elect or be elected."[43]

Since the majlis ash-shura deals with Islamic legislation, membership is restricted to those famliar with the Sharia. Hasan al-Banna felt that it should be open to "legists," or those with a broad general background, and heads of families, tribes, and other organized groups. Another of his associates stated that members should be "people most of whom would be knowledgeable in the law; the demands of the modern scientific world would make desirable the addition of specialists and technicians, but the final word would rest with the legists."[44]

Although Iran's new constitution establishes an Islamic Republic whose National Consultative Assembly is charged with implementing Quranic injunctions, the document also recognizes Iranian Zoroastrians, Jews, and Christians (Peoples of the Book) as ". . . the only recognized minorities, who, within the limits of the law, are free to perform their religious rites and ceremonies, and will act in personal matters and religious teachings in accordance with their religious regulations."[45] The constitution provides that, of the 270 seats in the Assembly, representatives of Zoroastrians and Jews will each have one, the Assyrian and Chaldean Christians will together have a representative, and Armenian Christians will elect two representatives.

Libya's president, Muaamar el-Qaddafi, has developed a "Third Universal Theory" of government with strong emphasis on the concept of shura. In the Third Universal Theory, conventional governmental institutions such as parliaments, parties, and central authorities, are to be replaced by "people's popular committees." In March 1979 Libya proclaimed that the country's government had ceased to exist and that the Libyan people would rule themselves through these popular congresses. The official name of the country was changed from Libyan Arab Republic to the Libyan *Jamahiriya,* meaning "The Libyan Masses." El-Qaddafi outlined his Third Theory in *The Green Book,* a small volume dividing the problems of the country into economic and political issues. In it el-Qaddafi states: "Popular congresses are the only means to achieve popular democracy. Any system of government other than popular congresses is undemocratic. All the prevailing systems of government in the world today are undemocratic, unless they adopt this method. Popular congresses are the end of the journey of the masses' movement in its quest for democracy."[46]

Prevailing systems of democracy, states el-Qaddafi, have failed to provide the masses with opportunity for participation. The "Utopia" of direct democracy has been replaced by representative assemblies, parties, coalitions, and plebiscites. "All led to the isolation of the people from political activity and to the plundering of the sovereignty of the people and the assumption of their authority by the successive and conflicting instruments of governing beginning with the individual, on through the class, the sect, the tribe, the parliament and the party . . ." The *Green Book* announces to the people "the happy discovery of the way to direct democracy, in a practical form . . . the problem of democracy in the world is finally solved. All that the masses need do now is to struggle to put an end to all forms of dictatorial rule in the world today, to all forms of what is falsely called democracy—from parliaments to the sect, the tribe, the class and to the one-party, the two-party and the multi-party systems."[47]

El-Qaddafi's model is similar to a syndicalist system in which citizens are divided into popular congresses by functional categories. In addition to affiliation with professional or occupational unions or syndicates, citizens are members of basic popular congresses or people's committees. Subjects discussed at lower levels will finally take shape in the General People's Congress, where the secretariats or popular congresses, syndicates, and unions meet. Legislative action is ratified in two directions: decisions of the General People's Congress are referred back to the popular congresses, people's committees, syndicates, and unions. The General People's Congress is described as an extraordinary assembly of representatives from the various groups throughout the country. In this way, el-Qaddafi states: ". . . the problem of the instrument of governing is, as a matter of fact, solved and dictatorial instruments will disappear. The people are the instrument of governing and the problem of democracy in the world is completely solved."[48]

The draft constitution proposed by Pakistani socialist students also places emphasis on "People's 'shuras' or people's councils at all levels."[49] It refers such tasks as tax collection, keeping law and order, providing education and health facilities, and road building to the shuras. The document cites countries like China, Russia, Yugoslavia, and Czechoslovakia which "have adopted the Islamic concept of consultation and administration."[50]

Social Justice

Most Muslim political theoreticians cite the Quran and the life of the Prophet as the source of their strong emphasis on concepts of social justice. The new Iranian constitution elaborates several specific obligations of the Islamic republic related to social justice. They include the requirement that the Islamic Republican Government provide "free education and physical training at all levels, and creation of facilities for the generalization of higher education";[51] "elimination of all kinds of despotism, autocracy and monopolism . . . participation of all the people in determining their political, economic, social and cultural destiny . . . elimination of inadmissible discriminations, and creation of fair possibilities for all, in all financial and moral fields and affairs . . . Laying the groundwork for a sound and just economy, based on Islamic regulations, aimed at creating comfort, elimination of poverty and all kinds of deprivations dealing with food, housing, jobs, hygiene, and generalization of social insurances . . . and expansion and strengthening of Islamic brotherhood and public cooperation among all of the people." The constitution includes specific requirements for social security benefits such as those for retirement, unemployment, old age, disability, medical care, education, and housing. One principle of the constitution states that: "A suitable dwelling, according to need, is the right of every Iranian person and family. The government is responsible for providing this, on a priority basis, to those who need it most, in particular the peasant and agricultural workers."[52]

The Pakistani socialist document mentioned above underscores social ownership of the means of production. This is based

". . . upon our belief that everything in this universe belongs to Allah and we are merely custodians of His wealth. As craftsmen, peasants, landowners, workers, teachers, journalists, students or industrialists, human beings are equal because we all are God's vicegerents on this earth. . . . No one is privileged to any monopoly or ownership, economic, social or political. This means an Islamic State is not a tool for the exploitation of the masses by one man or a group, but in fact, a means of providing security for all."[53]

"Since 'a worker is a friend of Allah' . . . the social substance of the Islamic State is to seek the well-being of those engaged in production and distribution. Thus, all communities combine to transform into a worldly paradise, the 'State of Allah.' The social ownership of the means of production becomes an inviolate basis of the Islamic order of the world. The promise of Paradise with inconceivable comforts and luxuries is a hint for us all to create in this world a replica of the things to come. This is the meaning of creating the Kingdom of God on earth. . . . The rich are provided more from Allah's wealth as a test to see if they will share it with others and thus retain the right of possession through benevolence."[54]

The Muslim Brothers also believed that all wealth belongs to society and ultimately to God. "Man merely utilizes it, within the limits of the law, in the role of 'steward.' The acquisition of wealth is possible only through 'work of any kind or variety.' " Employment specifically acknowledged as lawful by Islam includes hunting, fishing, mining, raiding, working at a wage for others, and the like. "All ultimately point to the fact that 'labour' is the only genuine foundation for possession. This means, in Islam, that there are no class distinctions based on material possession; whatever differences exist between men are of a mental and spiritual nature."[55]

Because labor is the foundation of property and endowed with both dignity and sacredness, the worker has certain duties as well as rights. "His relationship with his employer is governed by the principle governing all human relations—'a mutuality of duties and rights' based on mutual 'respect and sympathy' and ordered by the 'spirit of brotherhood.' He has the right to a healthy and clean home, wages adequate to provide the needs of life and 'punctually' paid, and limited hours of work. The worker is forbidden to 'allocate any part of his wages' to his leaders. In return for these rights he shall 'perform his work fully and faithfully,' thus respecting the rights of management and fulfilling his own responsibilities."[56]

In his *Green Book*, el-Qaddafi carries many of these concepts further, into a definitely socialist form of economic organization. He proceeds from the premise that: "Man's freedom is lacking if somebody else controls what he needs. For need may result in man's enslavement of man. Need causes exploitation. Need is an intrinsic problem and conflict grows out of the domination of man's needs."[57] In el-Quaddafi's ideal new society man works only for himself, for a socialist corporation, or to perform a public service for society. Economic activity must be productive, for satisfaction of social goals, not for accumulation of surplus profits. He states: ". . . no individual has the right to carry out economic activity in order to acquire more . . . than is necessary to satisfy his needs, because the excess amount belongs to other individuals. . . . if we allow economic activity to extend beyond the satisfaction of needs, one person will only have more than his needs by preventing another from obtaining his. The savings which are in excess of one's needs are another person's share of the wealth of society. . . . The final solution is the abolition of profit. But as profit is the driving force of economic activity, its abolition is not a decision that can be taken lightly. It must result from the development of socialist production which will be achieved if the satisfaction of the material needs of society is realised. The endeavor to increase profit will ultimately lead to its disappearance."[58]

The *Green Book* advocates division of production from both land and factory into three equal shares, one for the supplier of raw materials, one for the instrument of production, and one for the producer, or laborer. Terms like worker, employee, or toiler are to be replaced by the term "producer." Workers are changing from a multitude of ignorant toilers into a limited number of technicians, engineers, and scientists. "Consequently, Trade Unions will disappear to be replaced by professional and technical syndicates. . . . Through such scientific development, illiteracy will be eradicated and the ordinary worker as a temporal phenomenon will gradually disappear."[59]

Basic needs, such as housing, a vehicle for transportation, and land for agriculture, will be provided by the community. But no person may own more than one house, one vehicle, or more land than he can cultivate. Domestic servants, "a type of slave," will not be acceptable. "The house is to be served by its residents. But the solution to necessary house service should not be through servants, with or without wages, but through employees who can be promoted while performing their house jobs and can enjoy social and material safeguards like any employee in the public service."[60]

Finally, money and profit will disappear altogether. When society becomes fully productive, reaching the level where the material needs of all members are satisfied, "there will be no need for money." Profit will no longer be recognized, for "the mere recognition of profit removes the possibility of limiting it."[61]

El-Qaddafi's socialist Third Universal Theory carries the concept of equality in Islam much further than envisaged by more conservative theorists. Generally, the right of private ownership is recognized. "But unlike capitalism, which defends this absolutely (thus inspiring chaos), and communism, which denies it absolutely (thus restricting individual freedom), Islam recognizes the principle of possession but hedges it with controls in accordance with its primary concern 'the general welfare.' " Islam "ratifies that right of private property but along with it, it ratifies other principles which almost make it theoretical rather than practical."[62]

Islamic laws concerning inheritance derived from concepts of equitable property redistribution among heirs. By prescribed formulas for division of property, it was possible to set limits on large estates and to prevent monopolization of wealth. Other laws were intended to prevent usury and shady financial practices.

The Quran altered inheritance practices prevailing during the time of the Prophet. Primogeniture was abolished by the requirement that inheritances be divided among all children, both sons and daughters. The Quran prohibits the taking of interest on the principle that it is income not earned by one's own labor. "Everytime a Muslim lifts a morsel of food to his mouth, he should be able to answer affirmatively the question, 'Have I contributed to the human enterprise sufficiently to deserve what I am now receiving?' "[65] Since Islam prohibits interest, it allows only two forms of investment, through partnerships or through establishment of cooperative enterprises. These forms of investment ensure an equitable distribution of profits and losses. "The mode of investment serves—to a great extent—as an effective check against the concentration of wealth, which is the greatest evil of the capitalist economy. Wealth is so distributed over a very large number of individuals in the society that no injustice is done to anyone. Under the capitalist system, capitalists not only own the greater part of national wealth but also control the whole market and run it in their own interest. As a result, the systems of supply and pricing cannot function in a natural manner. They affect human life in such a way that none of its spheres remain unscathed.

"By prohibiting interest, Islam has struck at the very root of these evils. Under the Islamic system, everyone who invests his money has a share in the enterprise and its policy, bears the responsibility of both profit and loss, and is thus allowed to have his own way in business."[64]

According to Muhammad Asad, the deepest sociological lesson of Islam is that: " . . . there can be no happiness and strength in a society that permits some of its members to suffer undeserved want while others have more than they need. If the whole society suffers privations owing to extraordinary circumstances (as, for instance, happened to the Muslim community in the early days of Islam), such privations may become the source of spiritual strength and, through it, of future greatness. But if the available resources of a community are so unevenly distributed that certain groups within it live in affluence while the majority of the people are forced to use up all their energies in search of their daily bread, poverty becomes the most dangerous enemy of spiritual progress, and occasionally drives the whole community away from God-consciousness and into the arms of soul-destroying materialism."[65]

The Role of Non-Muslims

Islamic political theory assumes that the Muslim state will be established in areas with a predominantly Muslim population and that the overwhelming majority of citizens will be members of the Muslim community. Countries at the center of the Muslim world will have fewer non-Muslim citizens than those at the peripheries; thus the question of non-Muslims in the Islamic state will be less significant in the heartland than it will be at the peripheries. As we have seen, leadership of the Muslim state is reserved for those who are members of the faith. A man's religious beliefs are far more important in the Muslim state than the mere accident of his having been born or naturalized there. Asad writes that " . . . no ideological organization (whether based on religious or other doctrines) can afford to entrust the direction of its affairs to persons not professing its ideology."[65] Would the Soviet Union, he asks, permit a non-Communist to be given a key position?

While non-Muslims clearly play a secondary role in the Islamic state, they are guaranteed certain rights, as well as being required to fulfill certain obligations. Non-Muslims would be permitted to hold certain cabinet posts. Asad argues that under a presidential system of government, where ministers would be at the service of the Muslim head of state, the government should utilize, "on merit alone, all the best talent available in the country," regardless of the religious origin of the prospective office holder.

Non-Muslim citizens (People of the Book) would be required to participate in defending the state, according to Asad. Citing the history of early Islam, he states that the prophet never required non-Muslims living under Muslim protection to participate actively in his campaigns "waged in the defense of Islam." But neither did he forbid them to join Muslims in battle if they so desired. "The difference between Muslim and non-Muslim in this respect is that the former is bound by the commandments of his *religion* to sacrifice his life, if necessary, in a just war . . . whereas the non-Muslim citizen cannot under all circumstances be called upon to do the same. It may be presumed that the great majority of non-Muslim citizens would be willing, and even eager to play their part in the defense of a state that offers them full protection and guarantees all their civic rights: still, it is conceivable that some of these non-Muslims—especially Christians—might regard the bearing of arms as incompatible with their religious beliefs and, consequently, object to being drafted for military service; and to such 'conscientious objectors' would naturally apply the ordinance, 'There shall be no compulsion in religion.' "[67] Such conscientious objectors could be exempted if they paid a compensation tax called the *jizyah*, in lieu of military service. Asad asserts that this would be a tax fixed at a rate lower than the regular tax paid by Muslims, called the *zakat*. Because the zakat is a payment levied on Muslims for care of the indigent, it is considered a religious obligation, and is therefore not imposed on non-Muslim citizens.

Women

Fazlur Rahman states that the Quran's most important legal and general reforms were on the subject of women and slaves. "The Qur'an immensely improved the status of the woman in several directions but the most basic is the fact that the woman was given a full-fledged personality. The spouses are declared to be each other's 'garments': the woman has been granted the same rights over man as man has over his wife, except that man, being the earning partner, is a degree higher. Unlimited polygamy was strictly regulated and the number of wives limited to four, with the rider that if a husband feared that he could not do justice among several wives, he must marry only one wife. To all this was added a general principle that 'you shall never be able to do justice among wives no matter how desirous you are' (to do so). . . . The overall logical consequence of these pronouncements is a banning of polygamy under normal circumstances. Yet as an already existing institution polygamy was accepted on a legal plane, with the obvious guiding lines that when gradually social circumstances became more favourable, monogamy might be introduced. This is because no reformer who means to be effective can neglect the real situation and simply issue visionary statements. But the later Muslims did not watch the guiding lines of the Qur'an and, in fact, thwarted its intentions."[68]

Contemporary Muslim political theorists have recognized the growing importance of women's role in community public life and of the need to compensate women for past deprivations. The new Iranian Islamic constitution states that: "women, due to the greater oppression that they have borne under the idolatrous order [the Shah's regime], will enjoy more rights."[69] It gives to government the responsibility "for guaranteeing the rights of women in all areas according to Islamic standards and it must provide the following: 1. The creation of favorable environments for personal growth and restoring her material and intellectual rights. 2. Protection of mothers, especially during pregnancy and child rearing period, as well as the protection of orphans. 3. The formation of qualified courts for the protection of relatives and preservation of the family unit. 4. Creation of a special insurance for widows, old women and destitute women. 5. Granting guardianship to worthy mothers, to avoid envy, and in the absence of a lawful guardian."[70]

Pronouncements of the Muslim Brotherhood on women generally followed these guidelines. The organization proclaimed that women are the equals of men. Such discrimination as exists in inheritance, legal hearings, and prayer, is explained as a function of "the greater responsibility devolving on men and of the difference in the mental and emotional attributes of the sexes. Because mental power and emotional stability belong in larger measure to men, they are placed in a position of 'leadership'—'a fact' confirmed by history—and thus, 'one step' above women. This is a leadership of 'responsibility' and 'experience'—his are greater—and is not a priority of maleness over femaleness. Thus the only qualification to equality between male and female is a consequence of the 'practical' needs of living; this 'limited superiority,' one based on larger responsibility, is 'purely a dictate of worldly efficiency.' This does not preclude, e.g., in the family, that husband and wife 'work together' in their respective areas, sharing and consulting on joint problems 'to fulfill the mission of life.' "[71]

The Muslim Brothers claimed that they had no objection to women studying in universities or to their participation as professionals in agriculture, law, chemistry, and engineering. The most desirable of such professions would be medicine and teaching, occupations in which they would not be required to sacrifice their "femininity" and "sensitivity." Islam, claimed the Brothers, permits a woman to become a merchant, doctor, or lawyer, but: "Woman's real job is still the home and family: she creates 'for the son his manhood'; she is 'the spiritual source of love and kindness for her husband'; she alone creates 'the future of the nation.' These are the most noble of tasks. 'Religion does not forbid woman to work, but it does forbid her to flee from her natural place without excuse.' "[72]

International Relations

Muslims, as we have seen, perceive Islam as a universal system, eventually to include all mankind. Thus it was incumbent on Muslims to strive for propagation of the faith and to assist its spread to regions where it was still unknown. Following Muhammad's reign in Arabia there was great success in attaining this goal during the first centuries of the Muslim era.

As the Muslim empire expanded problems inevitably arose concerning relationships with non-Muslim states. Law concerning these relationships was based on a concept which divided the world into regions under control of Islam, *dar al-Islam,* and those not yet subjected to it—*dar al-harb,* the world of war. Islamic theory maintained that there could be no peace between the world of war and the world of Islam, although practical considerations could induce Muslim leaders to accept temporary armistice. According to the theory, territory once under Muslim rule could not be lawfully yielded to non-Muslim rule. It asserted that dar al-Islam included any area where at least one Muslim custom was still observed.

Since Muslim theorists believed that all mankind would eventually be governed by Islam, the law of nations was designed as a temporary institution, to be dispensed with once the non-Muslim regions were incorporated into dar al-Islam.

Some jurists devised a third and temporary division of the world, called *dar al-sulh*, world of peaceful truce, where there were non-Muslim nations which entered treaty relations with Islam based on terms acceptable to both parties. These theories were based on the experience of the Prophet in his dealings with groups in Arabia which had not yet accepted Islam, but with which he and his companions were not yet ready to wage war.

The first historical precedent for an agreement between Muslims and non-Muslims was the treaty negotiated by Muhammad after the hejira, or flight from Mecca to Medina. It was both a treaty with the non-Muslim groups in Medina, and also a constitution (the Constitution of Medina) setting out some of the basic ideas of the Islamic state in its formative stages. As Majid Khadduri points out, the Islamic law of nations " . . . is merely an extension of the law designed to govern the relations of the Muslims with non-Muslims, whether inside or outside the world of Islam. Strictly speaking, there is no Muslim law of nations in the sense of the distinction between modern municipal (national) law and international law based on different sources and maintained by different sanctions."[73]

The Constitution of Medina set precedents for relations between Muslims and non-Muslims because it elaborated ". . . the revolutionary concept of a state the foundations of which are laid on faith but which bestows oneness of community on those who do not belong to the same faith but are loyal to it in the political sense."[74] The document declared that the Muslims are a single community (*umma*) bound by their common faith. Muslims from the two hostile cities of Mecca and Medina became brothers, while breaking relations with their blood brothers who had not become Muslim. Muslims were thus bound together by the ideology of Islam, rather than by blood ties, tribal, or family connections. The treaty stated that the Jews of Medina, then a powerful group in the city hierarchy, were to be accepted as equals, entitled to practice their own faith free from interference of the Muslims. In exchange for this freedom, the Jews were to reciprocate with specific obligations to the Muslims, such as sharing with them costs of the war against unbelievers. The treaty recognized Muhammad as the final judge in settlement of disputes arising between Muslims and those with whom they signed the document.

As Islam spread during the Prophet's rule, similar agreements were signed with other Arab tribes in Arabia, and later with countries on the borders of dar al-Islam. Precedents established in the early days of Islam became part of the Sharia. "In practice, however, if the term 'law of nations' is taken to mean the sum total of the rules and practices of Islam's intercourse with other peoples, one should look further for evidences of the Muslim law of nations than to the conventional roots (*usul*) or sources of the Sharia. Some of the rules are to be found in the treaties which the Muslims concluded with non-Muslims, others in public utterances and official instructions of the caliphs to commanders in the field, which the jurists later incorporated in the canons; still others, the opinions and interpretations of the Muslim jurists on matters of foreign relations. Analyzed in terms of the modern law of nations, the sources of the Muslim law of nations conform to the same categories defined by modern jurists and the Statute of the International Court of Justice, namely, agreement, custom, reason, and authority."[75]

Majid Khadduri has summarized certain general characteristics of Muslim treaties with non-Muslims. They were usually quite general and brief, without details of implementation. Because they were frequently simple and brief, they were often vague. The preamble of every treaty consisted of the so-called *basmala* (in the name of Allah, etc.). The preamble listed the names of the representatives of the concerned parties. It often ended with a list of witnesses present at the drafting. There were both permanent and temporary treaties. The former were signed with those People of the Book who were protected by Islam and who lived under its jurisdiction. Temporary treaties were signed with those in dar al-harb. They temporarily suspended the state of *jihad* or struggle. Muslim jurists usually limited the time span of temporary treaties. Some held that a peace treaty with the enemy should not exceed ten years. Others placed even shorter time limits on such agreements. Muslim rulers tended to regard the terms of treaties as religious obligations to be strictly observed. Even when jurists expressed reluctance about such agreements, once they were concluded, the terms were to be strictly observed until the date of termination.[76]

During the era of Islam's expansion, when Muslims anticipated that the faith and its political-legal system would become universal, peaceful relations with the non-Muslim world were expected to be only temporary. Relations with dar al-harb were more often governed by the concept of jihad, commonly, but incorrectly, translated as holy or religious war. A more accurate and literal translation is an effort or a striving, an effort or striving in Allah's path. In the Quran this injunction commands:

"O ye who believe! Shall I guide you to a gainful trade which will save you from painful punishment? Believe in Allah and His Apostle and carry on warfare (jihad) in the path of Allah with your possessions and your persons. That is better for you. If ye have knowledge, He will forgive your sins, and will place you in the Gardens beneath which the streams flow, and in fine houses in the Gardens of Eden: that is the great gain."[77]

Muslim theologians have interpreted jihad to mean exertion to advance the faith by either peaceful or warlike methods. In early revelations of the Quran, Muhammad emphasized persuasion, warning the Meccans against idolatry and urging them to worship Allah. After the hejira to Medina, jihad is expressed more in terms of strife, with emphasis on war against the unbelievers. Later, jurists interpreted the Prophet's jihads, or struggles, by four different ways: by his heart, his tongue, his hands, and by the sword.

Muslim interpreters of the Quran assert that the Prophet prohibited war except for defensive purposes or for propagation of the faith against non-believers who refused the message of Allah. According to Hadith, the Prophet ordered his followers "to fight the polytheists until they say: 'There is no god but God.' " Jihad was also sanctioned against People of the Book who refused to pay the poll tax.

By the thirteenth century there were significant changes in dar al-Islam. A process of fragmentation into several Islamic states had begun, and the unity of Islam was no longer a politcial reality. Furthermore, parts of dar al-Islam fell to the non-Islamic world and Western Christian influences were penetrating Muslim states. As Muslim rulers abandoned the objective of establishing a universal Islamic order there was a tendency to sign treaties with non-Muslim states based on an equal relationship, and on mutual recognition. A classic example of the new balance in relationships was the treaty signed in 1535 between France and the Ottoman Empire. It recognized equality in the relationships between the Ottoman sultan and the King of France. It provided for a "valid and sure peace" during the lives of the two monarchs, and granted reciprocal rights to the subjects of each monarch in the territory of the other. A significant innovation was extension of the time limit of the treaty from the conventional ten years to the lifetime of the signatories. Another was exemption from the poll tax of non-Muslims who resided in dar al-Islam more than a year.

By the seventeenth and eighteenth centuries, Islam was no longer a superior force in international politics, but had begun a sharp and steady decline vis-à-vis the West. The decline culminated with the collapse and disintegration of the Ottoman empire during World War I, the division of most of its territories among Western Christian states, and the disappearance of Islam as a political force in international relations. The end of World War I found most of the Muslim world under the political domination of European Christian powers and saw the virtual end of the division between dar al-Islam and dar al-harb as a significant political factor.

To the extent that terms such as dar al-Islam, dar al-harb and jihad had political significance in the Muslim world, they represented either historical memories, or aspirations by Muslim peoples living within European empires for political and/or cultural independence. Thus the Muslim Brotherhood in Egypt perceived the struggle against British occupation as a jihad and invited King Farouk and his prime minister in 1946 to call on the nation to join the struggle. The Brothers also participated in the Palestine campaign by sending volunteer military units to assist the Palestinian Arabs in the "jihad" against the Zionists.

Jihad represented to the Brothers not only the military struggle against British occupation or Zionist penetration of Islamic territories but a struggle against corrupting influences of Western ideologies and values. Although the Western democracies had much to commend them, particularly with regard to respect for individual freedom and the rights of workers to protect their interests, democracy also led to corruption of individuals and thus of societies. "An excess of 'individualism' has led to licence and has set man against man and class against class; it has led, too, to moral irresponsibility, 'degeneracy,' and 'social chaos,' all of which have precipitated crisis in the home—the debasement of women and the weakening and destruction of the family. On another plane, democracy has become synonymous with capitalism and its exploitive basis of legally recognized usury. And, finally, in the leading democracy of the West, failure has marked efforts to solve the 'race issue on the basis of equality and justice'; America has become the defender and leader of 'the empire of the white man.' "[78]

The Brotherhood was equally critical of the communist world for its "atheisim," its "political tryanny," and its "international dictatorship." The ". . . Russian 'concept of equality' is so materialistic as to be meaningless; and the guiding principle of the system is 'destructive' and 'incites to revolution.' "

The common denominator of all the Western systems is materialism, greed, and tyranny. Hasan al-Banna summed up these negative views: " 'The civilization of the West', proudly strong in its science, and for a period able to subjugate the world, is now 'in bankruptcy and in decline,' its political fundamentals destroyed by dictatorship, its economic systems racked by crisis [written in 1936], its social order decaying. 'Revolution is in process everywhere.' 'The people are perplexed'; greed, materialism, and oppression have destroyed the relations between states . . . 'all humanity' is 'tortured' and 'miserable.' Leadership of the world, first Eastern, moved westwards with the Greeks and Romans and eastwards again following the Semitic prophets [sic]. And finally with the Renaissance it passed into the hands of a 'tyrannical' and 'oppressive' West. The time has come for the East to rise again."[79]

The Muslim Brothers, like Islamic revivalists in Iran today, perceive the retreat of Muslim civilization before Western civilization and the need for an internal jihad of the spirit to resist continued incursions of their lands. "Banna warned his followers early and often that 'formal political independence' was worthless unless accompanied by 'intellectual, social, and cultural independence.' And one of his most frequently quoted sayings . . . was 'Eject imperialism from your souls, and it will leave your lands.' " Another writer ". . . deplored 'this age, created by the cultural invasion, which bears Muslim names, but has not a Muslim heart or a Muslim mind.' 'The cultural invasion . . . makes Muslims ignorant of their religion and loads their minds with limited truths, then leaves their hearts a vacuum.' . . . [He] warns the Brothers that 'spiritual and mental imperialism is the true danger' for unlike military or political imperialism which inspires opposition, this type dulls, calms, and deceives its victims. 'Holy war' must be declared against 'the apparatus which directs the operation of deception': the 'modern' techniques of the imperialism of the 'free world'—foundations, technical aid, UNESCO, and the 'pens and tongues' of the 'people's democracies.' "[80]

Muhammad Asad also warns against the cultural institutions of the West, more dangerous than military occupation or political domination. He berates Muslims who have found false gods in science or pure reason; who have made "right" and "wrong" purely relative terms, "to be interpreted arbitrarily according to one's personal or communal needs, which, in their turn, are subject to the continuous changes in one's socio-economic environment."[81] Furthermore, he writes,

Ever since the Crusades, Islam has been misrepresented in the West, and a deep distrust—almost hatred—of all Islamic propositions has become part and parcel of the Western cultural heritage. The Westerners see in the tenets of Islam not only a denial of many of the fundamental beliefs of their own religion but also a political threat. Under the influence of their historical memories of the centuries of passionate warfare between the Muslim world and Europe, they attribute to Islam—quite unjustifiably—an inherent hostility toward all non-Muslims; and so they fear that a revival of the Islamic spirit, as manifested in the idea of the Islamic state, might revive the slumbering strength of the Muslims and drive them to new aggressive adventures in the direction of the West. To counteract such a possible tendency, the Westerners are doing their utmost to prevent a resurgence of political power in Muslim countries and a restoration of Islam to its erstwhile dominant position in Muslim social and intellectual life. Their means of combat are not merely political; they are cultural as well. Through the instrumentality of Western schools and of Western oriented methods of education in the Muslim world, the distrust of Islam as a social doctrine is being systematically planted in the minds of the younger generation of Muslim men and women; and the principal weapon in this campaign to discredit Islam is being supplied, unconsciously, by the reactionary elements within our own society. By insisting that the political forms and procedures of a contemporary Islamic state must strictly follow the pattern evolved in the early period of Islam (an insistence for which there is not the slightest warrant in Quran or Sunnah), these self-appointed "guardians" of Muhammad's Message made it impossible for many educated Muslims to accept the *shari'ah* as a practical proposition for the political exigencies of our time. By representing the idea of *jihad*, in clear contradiction of all Qur'anic injunctions, as an instrument of aggressive expansion of Muslim rule over non-Muslim territories, they sow fear in the hearts of the non-Muslims and fill many righteous Muslims with disgust at the thought of the injustice which such a tendency so obviously implies. And, finally, by claiming (again, without any warrant in Qur'an or Sunnah) that the *shari'ah* imposes on us the duty to discriminate, in all social aspects of life, between the Muslim and non-Muslim citizens of an Islamic state to the detriment of the non-Muslim minorities, they make it impossible for the minorities to bear with equanimity the thought that the country in which they live might become an Islamic state.[82]

While most of the Muslim world, using Islamic justification, has joined the Arab countries in rejecting the Egyptian-Israeli peace treaty, theologians at Cairo's prestigious al-Azhar University claimed support for the document through Islamic precedents. Shortly after the treaty was signed in March 1979, Egypt's leading cleric, the Sheikh of al-Azhar, issued a fatwa published in one of the country's leading newspapers, headlined: "The treaty with Israel does not include anything incompatible with the Koran or the Sunna. It did not surrender any rights or agree to occupation of any land. Instead it liberated land and regained rights."[83]

The fatwa drew heavily on traditional Islamic sources and precedents, including Hadith, Sunna, Quran, and examples from the Prophet's life to sustain the argument. The first treaties signed by Muhammad with non-Muslims at Medina and Hudeibah were cited as evidence of legitimacy in establishing peaceful relations, including economic and social dealings, with non-Muslims. In this instance the early historical precedents were particularly significant because they were signed with Jewish tribes in Medina. In more general terms, the fatwa justified the agreement because Islam has always been "the religion of peace and tranquility, of friendship and brotherhood and not of war and hostility." Islam's use of the sword, the fatwa argued, was not to dominate, occupy, or conquer others, but to spread the word of God. Thus, it is argued, the Quran has forbidden the faithful from waging aggressive wars—only those necessary for preservation of the faith are tolerated. Even if war has begun, peaceful offers should be considered. "If they lean toward peace, you too should lean toward peace," states the Quran.

Although Egypt resisted Israel's occupation of Arab lands in four wars, states the fatwa, when Egypt was at the height of its power and dignity after the victory in the 1973 war, it offered peace to Israel. "Peace would give the Arabs breathing space from the long and futile war that seemed to have no end in sight." President Sadat achieved a victory in peace, as he did in his Sinai military victory, by persevering in his argument with the Israelis until they accepted peace and agreed to evacuate the occupied land of Egypt over a ten-year period.

When the Prophet made peace with the Jews in Medina, the fatwa recalls, he kept his promises, for Islam prohibits making such agreements for the purpose of trickery or merely to gain time. "Fulfill your obligations to God and do not go back on your promises. God made you the guardian of his word and he can see what you do," states the Quran. If this treaty with Israel is examined in light of the rules of Islam, Sheik al-Azhar observes, "we find that it is based on the Quran and the Sunna, and conforms to all the various schools of Islamic thought, for it liberated a sizeable part of Islamic lands and many Muslim citizens, returning to them their freedom and wealth which had been drained by our adversaries."

Although it has been said by critics of the treaty that it violated Egypt's pacts with other Arab states because it is a unilateral agreement, this is not true, according to the fatwa. There is now a consensus among the Arabs that only a peaceful solution is practical because war has failed. Because other Arab leaders failed to utilize the way of peace, it was incumbent on someone to take the initiative, and thus Egypt acted unilaterally, becoming the "trustee of the public interest." In support of the Prophet's injunction, "your brother right or wrong," it is the sacred duty of every Arab ruler and all the Muslim ulema to rally behind the Egyptian President, who has been fighting to liberate and regain lands and places sacred to Islam. It is the duty of Muslims to give him their support, not to make obstacles, because Sadat is working for all Islam. Therefore it is, according to the al-Azhar sheikh, improper for any Muslim to undermine Sadat's work.

In this essay we have seen that there is a wide range of Islamic perspectives concerning internal structure of the Islamic system, its laws and government, and its relations with non-Muslims. Although most Muslim political theorists build their doctrines from the relatively narrow base of the Sharia, over the centuries these doctrines and theories have evolved in such a variety of national and cultural contexts that they now can justify reactionary, conservative, liberal, or radical ideologies. This diversity of political and social ideologies can be traced back to the fundamental, uncomplicated, and relatively simple pronouncements of the Prophet. They can be used to justify and explain either war or peace with Israel, establishment of a strongly centralized or a loosely confederated state, strict confinement of women or their open participation in public life, a social system in which economic power is held by a few, or one in which there is an equitable diffusion of material wealth through all sectors of society, restrictions on participation of non-Muslims in the life of an Islamic state, or their encouragement to play an active role at all but the highest levels. What is even more significant is that in recent decades the elite in Muslim countries has been seeking, more and more, an Islamic rationale for the decisions they are making for their societies, and that as these societies become increasingly dissatisfied with Western models and modes, pressures on the elite have grown to seek Islamic solutions to the many problems they face.

Islam and Development in Muslim Countries

by Richard U. Moench

Introduction: Obstacles to an Understanding

There is a scenario by which Americans seem to interpret events in the Islamic world, and it goes something like this: the United States was never a colonial presence in the Middle East, yet its sincere attempts today to bring peace between Israel and its Arab neighbors are met increasingly with verbal hostility on the part of Muslim nations, and disaffection even among some who were formerly close friends of the United States — Jordan, Pakistan, Saudi Arabia, and Morocco. Only Egypt stands firmly on our side, safe for the moment from Soviet expansionist plans. This growing tension is linked to a phenomenon called "Islamic revival," which is actually causing the tension. This happens because of our efforts to provide aid for economic deveopment in the Middle East. Such aid has contributed to rapid modernization in the area, and that, in turn, to frustration and resentment on the part of tradition-oriented Middle Easterners unable to cope with so rapid an introduction into the twentieth century. This frustration and resentment becomes directed against the sources of this rapid modernization, their government and the United States.

The Iranian revolution is the most publicized case in which all the elements of the above scenario are present.

If by this scenario we measure events and evaluate what people in Muslim countries are saying to us, then the scenario poses an obstacle to our understanding of recent events in that part of the world. This lack of understanding has been clearly demonstrated in the Iranian crisis. Instead of expressing sympathy for the Iranian masses held in check by a harsh police state while a middle class became wealthy, modern, and "Western" to the point of losing touch completely with the underclasses, the news media here suggested that the trouble in Iran was the too liberal policies of the

49

Shah! From this we are led to believe that there are two struggles in Iran, one in the name of Muhammad born in the mind of an angry ayatollah in exile, the other in the name of Karl Marx born in Moscow. In fact, both struggles rise from the same source.

A second obstacle to our understanding is not, as in the case of the first, based on historical interpretation but on what all agree to be United States Middle East policy. The disagreement comes with respect to the legitimacy of this policy, which claims that our national interest revolves around three concerns: oil, the protection of Israel, and the containment of communism. The reason this poses an obstacle to our understanding is that all events are inevitably interpreted in the light of these three concerns, to the exclusion of any awareness that the national interests of Middle Eastern countries do not mirror ours, and that this is a source of confusion, bitterness, and open anger directed toward the United States. This anger in a real sense is a *cause* rather than an effect of much that has been called "Islamic revival."

A third obstacle to an understanding arises as a product of the second. Looking at the Middle East in terms of great-power competition frequently ends in the view that the Muslim countries, as indeed all Third World countries, eventually will have to make a commitment to join the "free world" (implying a capitalist strategy for their national development) or the communist world (implying a socialist strategy for development). The possibility of a third option is rejected outright. This "two worlds" attitude is an obstacle preventing us from hearing all but the most strident voices in the Middle East, and with respect to those, it causes us to misinterpret their message.

A fourth obstacle arises from the third. A "two worlds" view of international events inevitably tends to color (red rather than green) our observations of the popularity of socialism among Muslim countries. At one time or another, either the government or a dominant political party of Syria, Iraq, Egypt, Tunisia, Algeria, Pakistan, Afghanistan, and South Yemen have claimed socialism as the preferred path to national development.

A failure to understand the basis of the popularity of socialism presents us with a false dilemma: should we support Islamic movements because they are strongly anti-Soviet, or should we fear them because they develop anti-American sentiments and, by opposing modernization, tend to perpetuate the very conditions on which instability and revolution thrive?

This last assumption amounts to a fifth obstacle to understanding, one which has received pedigreed support from the academy in the form of a corrupted version of Max Weber's thesis[1] relating rational economic behavior to Protestant beliefs. In its corrupted form, other religions are viewed as major contributors to the inability of non-European countries to develop economically. This has led to biased histories of the relations between Christian Europe and the Muslim Middle East, which are available to mystify further the serious reader searching in his public library for clarification of events such as we have been witnessing in past months.

Orientalist literature has contributed to a final obstacle to our understanding the notion of the unity of Islam and of the Muslim world. Such writings do not claim the homogeneity of Islam so much as they ignore its heterogeneity by describing a construct called "Islam" and illustrating it with examples chosen from observations made in countries ranging from Morocco to Indonesia and covering nearly fourteen centuries. The result is a patchwork Islam that exists nowhere. The implication of unity comes from phrases such as "Islam distinguishes" and "Islam rejects," when they actually mean "Sunni Muslims in Iraq distinguish . . ." or "Hanbali doctrine rejects."

The common denominator of Islam does not go beyond the minimal definition of being Muslim and following the Quran. In addition to sectarian differences that separate Sunni and Shiite, in addition to the special practices and beliefs of the different Sufi orders, in addition to the contrasting interpretations of what is lawful by the four Sunni schools of Islamic jurisprudence — in addition to all these sources of variation there are those which divide Muslims into political factions based on the positions they take vis-a-vis Islam's role in the development of their countries. Here it is not sufficient to distinguish modern from traditional. At the very least it is necessary to recognize four distinct approaches, four interpretations of Islam's proper role in modernization. We shall refer to these as traditionalist, fundamentalist, modernist, and secularist.[2]

Because the core of Islam is a legal system, it has been accumulating tradition over the centuries. The guardians of this tradition and the real Islamic traditionalists in the legal sense are the doctors learned in Islamic law, the *ulema*. Although generally defenders of the status quo and reactionary in the face of change, occasionally ulema splinter into "progressive" and "traditional" factions. Since decisions by the ulema have added to Islamic tradition over the centuries, their authority and authenticity are often challenged, especially if recent.

One faction who challenge modern interpretation by the ulema are the "fundamentalists," such as the Jamaat-i-Islami party in Pakistan and the now illegal Ikhwan al-Muslimin (Muslim Brotherhood) in Egypt and Syria, who opposed nationalism on religious grounds. Fundamentalists are reformers who conclude that the plight of Muslim societies today derives from impurities that have crept into Islam, especially from Western thought. They accept the authenticity only of the Quran and the *Sunna*.

Not all reformers are fundamentalists. Equally devoted to reform are the "modernists." These agree with the fundamentalists that much of the content of Islamic law should be expunged. Their reasoning is as follows: legal decisions in Islam are never made in advance of a need for a decision, therefore they refer to real rather than hypothetical situations. These historical situations may have made such decisions valid in the past, but the strictures are no longer valid, and should not be accepted dogmatically.

Modernists believe that an Islamic core exists containing truths that are eternal and applicable to all ages, including the modern age. Stripped of historically specific content, their Islam consists of the fundamental messages conveyed by the Prophet, guidelines so general as to be compatible with the demands of modern technological society. They differ from the fundamentalists in that the latter insist that Islamic sources be the exclusive source of legitimacy for all innovations. Thus fundamentalists may find themselves in support of socially progressive changes where scriptural legitimacy can be demonstrated, but opposed to comparable changes where no such legitimacy can be found, as in, for example, the status of women. Modernists do not insist on this stricture, nor regard the coexistence of positive legislation with *Sharia* as contradictory. But modernists have difficulties in gaining acceptance of their positions. "Modern" in the Middle East has for the past century become a synonym of "Western." Though today modernists are often critical of the West, they are accused of being apologists for Islam, and of applying criteria for the reform of Islam that will make the religion compatible with Western values.[3] From abroad they are equally misunderstood, since to us the essence of modernism is secularism — Western thought became modern when it freed itself of theology — and Islamic modernists insist on a major role for Islam.

Secularists are thus distinguished from modernists by the insistence by the former of a strict separation of church and state in the Western manner. Reform is unimportant as long as modernization and development are carried out according to practical scientific principles, regardless of their origins.

A further source of diversity is that which arises from the fact that Islam is a literate tradition, yet the masses of its followers are illiterate. Nice distinctions of some importance to an urban *tariqa* (Sufi brotherhood) composed of businessmen would not be perceived by those attending a village mosque. For the Arab peasant as for the Pakistani fisherman, Islam is the source of legitimacy for every right act in his daily life, indistinguishable from what we would call his culture. It is therefore not possible for him to discuss his religion apart from customary practices. By comparing Islamic practices in different cultures, anthropologists have enriched our sense of the heterogeneity of the religion and the diversity of the cultures. The conclusion to be drawn is that Islam has everywhere conformed to local belief, even while Islamicizing these beliefs. The existence of a literate tradition never insures standardization among millions of illiterate followers.

If, then, Islam offers a model for social life, it is a variable one. If underlying its multiplicity is a unity, this unity itself is a kind of dynamic contradiction: disciplined duty to God based on faith, on the one hand; reason and responsibility toward the realities of the material world, on the other. In most Muslim societies, little is shared between middle classes and masses except Islam. Still, the bridge is fragile, for the literate classes pre-empt the tradition of Islamic rationality, while the illiterate content themselves with faith and duty. This does not entitle us to assume that the primary distinction is one of devotion. The use of alcohol, for example, probably occurs more frequently among the middle class because of its cost and its availability in cities. If the observations of anthropologists and the rare others who have been willing to spend substantial periods in villages and camps are reliable, fellahin and Bedouins both maintain a fierce devotion to their religion while breaking most of its tenets daily by acts which would appall the petty bureaucrat, scrupulous in his observance of his religion.

Should Islamic revival be a genuine phenomenon (we who are regularly subjected to media events have a right to ask if it is), what can we expect of the consequences for the continued modernization of Muslim nations? Admittedly, this is not the kind of question that first springs to mind when Islam is mentioned to an average American. He rightly wishes to know what Islam is, and how it affects a people so that they become hostile toward the United States, take our citizens hostage, weaken our economy with oil price rises, and threaten our legitimate concerns in the area. Still we believe that the question of the role a revived Islam will play in the development strategies selected by Muslim nations is a valid starting point for understanding today's events in the Middle East, for every Muslim nation shares one thing: its highest priority is the development of a modern society. And even a cursory look at recent events involving student movements, the adoption of modest dress codes, even national revolutions, will provide a sharp contrast with the consensus of impressions of Muslim writers of the 1960s, who saw an irreversible trend toward secularism as characterizing the modernization of the Middle East.

The "Islamic revival" is still largely a media event. Scholars are just beginning to disassemble the phenomena. It is likely that at least three movements will emerge: (1) the increased use of Islamic symbols as a form of protest, especially by students and young dissidents, for example those who oppose their government's policies as courting dependency on the West; (2) the use of Islamic symbols for mobilizing revolutionary movements; (3) the increasing participation of popular strata in politics. The Arab writers who agreed, in their 1965 articles published in *The Modernization of the Arab World*,[4] that the direction of the future was inevitably secular were reflecting a secularism of the middle classes, not of the masses. Consequently, the political involvement of the masses was bound to make any new movement more Islamic, without any new dedication to Islam on the part of either class.

In this chapter we shall review the arguments, insofar as possible those put forth by Muslim writers, for reinterpreting Muslim attitudes toward capitalism and socialism as alternative paths to development. We then pose the question, in the event that an independent Third Path becomes both necessary and viable, what will be the relationship of Islam to development? Is it possible that Islam could become an ideology of development? If Islam is a rigid, medieval religion (and many writers have said so), then it must ultimately constitute an obstacle to development, a substitute for rational planning. Not all Muslim intellectuals are yet ready to con-

Twentieth-century anthropology in America contributed to this second scenario a theory of cultural determinism (to replace racial determinism) to explain societal differences; and it rejected for a period of fifty years the idea of progress as too subjective. Thus the great myth that innovative change requires only proper motivation, and that it is the role of ideology to supply this motivation, found a new American respectability.

Western-educated Muslim scholars, and the products of the new secular education at home, followed their mentors in blaming their cultures for the backwardness of their societies, and Islam as the traditionally designated source of all legitimacy came to be viewed as the primary obstacle preventing the modernization of Middle Eastern societies. Islamic modernists today remain critical of the traditional doctrinaire positions as impediments to development. Thus, Professor Fazlur Rahman writes:

"Now the orthodox Muslim theological formulations are almost out-and-out predeterministic, presenting a rather odd contrast to the moral freshness and fervor that the Qur'an seeks to evoke"[5]

Was Islam truly an impediment to the development of economic rationality and modernization in the Muslim countries? Is it today? Since Weber, economic rationality has usually been interpreted as synonymous with the term "capitalism." Has the faith of Muslims in Islam's principles affected their economic striving? Has it channeled efforts in directions contrary to the needs of economic development? What is the evidence?

Western scholars familiar with Islam point to proscriptions against *riba* (usury, but in some interpretations, interest in any form) as a disincentive to rational commercial practices. Others point out the high proportion of non-Muslims who have traditionally filled the position of professional moneylender (Jews in Morocco, Christians in Egypt, etc.) in Muslim countries, drawing the conclusion that their religion kept Muslims from pursuing such trades. Still others have referred to the *haj* as a drain on income which might otherwise have been invested in productive activity. Many non-scholars have assumed that devout Muslims have always been hostile to the reception of foreign ideas, without which progressive change is rarely possible. Was Islam a major factor in the Muslim world's failure to modernize even after Western contact?

The last accusation deserves reflection. Islam has periodically in its history openly and actively incorporated outside ideas which led to the enrichment of Islamic jurisprudence and philosophy. The question, then, is why should there be such great sensitivity about foreign (especially Western) ideas, starting with the late nineteenth century? The response among Muslim thinkers to the secularism of modern Western thought varied from enthusiastic acceptance by lay Muslims to fear and hostility by the ulema. Explicit imitation of the West in development strategies was rare. Only Turkey under Kemal Attaturk adopted wholly secular laws with a constitution patterned after the Swiss, and a policy of separation of church and state. The hostility of the religious establishment and of fundamentalist movements increased with increased Westernization, and finally, Christian missionizing. Compared with those periods when Islam, at its peak of power and glory, digested whole feasts of classical, Byzantine, and medieval Christian philosophy without encountering any threat to its collective identity, foreignisms since the nineteenth century have posed a genuine threat to the Muslim identity. The early receptivity of the educated elite to modernization, the close identity of modernization with Westernization, and of Westernization with secularism, all served to aggravate further the Muslim's sensibilities to the backwardness of his culture and his beliefs. Even with reform movements, where reformers insisted that *ijtihad* be reopened, there was hostility among fundamentalists to the inclusion of non-Islamic ideas for consideration. Western ideas, associated with the imperialism of their messengers, could not be considered dispassionately.

As for the actual effects of Islamic institutions which today appear "medieval" (and, in origin, frequently are), two separate questions arise. The first is one of discovering the rationale at the time and the historical context in which it was adopted. The second is the question of the ways in which these dicta have been interpreted as the context changed, and how they presently affect behavior. To discover the existence of a seemingly archaic injunction is no more to condemn the vitality of Islam than would the discovery in modern American statutes of a law forbidding the tethering of sheep in front of the courthouse condemn our own legal system as archaic.

Much of the literature on Islam has in fact adopted the apologist's approach, a trend that seems to have strengthened the position of fundamentalist Islam, for after encountering volumes of argument that Islam does not really mean what it says, one is inclined to pay serious respect to those who say "Yes, it does!" Reformist writers have dared to be critical of the Islamic traditions incorporated over recent centuries but not of the earlier period in which

Islam as a political system, as well as a cultural and religious system, was in the process of being assembled, which has been romanticized as an ideal state proving that once upon a time, at least, Islam "worked."

In Western scholarship, one work stands out because it challenges the view that Islam is responsible for the economic backwardness of the Middle East. Although regarded by some as apologetic, and criticized by others for its methodology (defending an entity called "Islamic civilization" without demonstrating its unity over time and space), the work entitled *Islam and Capitalism,* by Maxime Rodinson, the French orientalist and historian of Islam, deserves special mention. Selecting evidence from an area extending from Iran to Morocco and a time span of more than twelve centuries, Rodinson concludes that Islam has never proved incompatible with capitalism and cannot be the cause for the backwardness of the Muslim world. He defends his thesis with two sorts of evidence. First, he examines the prescriptions and proscriptions of the Quran and the *Hadiths*, and discovers nothing that could be considered a barrier to the development of commercial or financial capitalism — nothing, that is, by which interpretations provided by at least some legal experts of Islam (ulema) would have made the transaction of commerce impossible or even difficult. Mecca, the birthplace of Islam, was a center of medieval commerce, and trade has remained a respected occupation throughout Islam's history. Money and profits have never been despised under Islam; indeed, the Prophet commended productivity over prayer and piety, and subsequent theologians have tempered antimaterialist arguments with ones that emphasize Islam's ideal of moderation (excessive spirituality is as destined to failure as excessive preoccupation with worldly matters).

Of course, early Islam shared with medieval Christianity philosophical doubts regarding the good and bad effects of wealth; but to the degree that they differed, Islam seems to have accepted wealth, if accompanied by responsibility, as less of a threat to morality than did the medieval Christian church. Islam's expansion, especially eastward, was largely the product of missionizing traders; the pious Muslim merchant is a stock character in the Indies.

Rodinson finds sufficient evidence to satisfy him that riba (ban on usury) was never a ban on profit-taking, and even interest was condoned by the religious establishment for certain transactions, certain purists to the contrary notwithstanding. What was proscribed was unreasonable profit and interest from moneylending.

Yet Muslims engaged in moneylending, even while non-Muslims claimed to monopolize the occupation. Modern Muslim writers sometimes try to blame colonialism for the introduction of usury into Muslim countries, though its existence in pre-Islamic Mecca is certain.

Even a religious ban on interest for money lent apparently had little effect on the *de facto* charging of interest on financial transactions, through a universally known set of circumventions of riba involving fictional sales and resales of token objects, thus satisfying the letter of the law, if not its spirit.

The Quran, Rodinson argues, warned not against the evil of profit-seeking but against false representation, speculation, and corrupt practices. Thus Islamic law disapproved of price-fixing and other acts that interfered with the operation of the market, a position which would have won the support of Adam Smith and Milton Friedman. As to the accusation that faith is the enemy of reason, Rodinson can only conclude that with Islam it is faith in a "reasonable message," that it is understandable through human reason, a claim that neither the Old Testament nor the New Testament can make:

> The ideology of the Koran is thus seen to accord a greater role to reasoning and rationality then is found in the ideologies that are reflected in the Old and New Testaments; to invoke the idea of predestination more or less to the same degree as we find in those scriptures, while clearly exhorting men to be active in their individual and social lives; and, finally, to subordinate the technique of magic to the divine will exactly as in the two other books of revealed truth, thereby safeguarding men's ability to frustrate this technique, however cleverly it may have been employed.[7]

Rodinson in the above is saying not that religiously derived rationality is employed in both Islam and Christianity to expose the unreality of magical claims, but rather, that religious rationality accepts the existence of magical powers but subordinates them to God's permission. Thus Islam shares with Judeo-Christian scriptures a hostility toward magic, while with respect to fatalism, nothing supports its association with Islam, though it appears in Muslim populations. This is a view contradicted by Muslim reformers[5] who wish to distinguish between the Quranic exhortation to reason and later doctrinaire and dogmatic Islamic traditions defended by the establishment as law. It is possible to sympathize, nonetheless, with Rodinson's point. One frequently encounters fatalism among Muslim peasants, among Hindu peasants, and Buddhist peasants. Is fatalism then religiously inspired or is it a factor of the economically marginal producers in an uncertain environment? It is not sufficient to note that the Egyptian fellah invokes God, but to record carefully under what circumstances he does so, and whether or not he works any less hard because of having done so. The hopeless invoke God; so do the hopeful, the trader exhorting his customer to return.

The second body of evidence utilized by Rodinson to test the Weberian thesis that Islam prevented the rise of rational economic organization in Muslim countries comes not from Islamic documents at all, but from secular history: to what extent had Muslim countries proved able to develop capitalist institutions comparable to those of the West? He notes that the existence of merchant and financial capital and its institutions are regarded in medieval Europe as "preconditions" for the rise of capitalism, and proceeds to show that these were developed to about the same extent in the Muslim world. He goes so far as claiming the existence of "capitalist sectors" in medieval Muslim societies, distinguishing a "capitalist sector" from "capitalism" in the following way: "capitalism" requires that the entire economy be dominated by a single (capitalist) mode of production, while a capitalist sector may exist in societies which are feudal, tribal, or whatever — that is, societies characterized by several modes of production, one non-dominant one being capitalist. The concept of "mode of production" is of course Marxist, but Rodinson's characterization of a "capitalist sector" includes the Weberian sense of "rationality" in the commercial and financial transactions. In the sense in which the economic historian Karl Polanyi used the term, "rational" economic relations are no longer "embedded" in social institutions. Obviously, most transactions in the rural Middle East today, and in domestic relations nearly everywhere, are constrained by kinship affiliations, tribal affiliations, voluntary association affiliations, all of which resist being reformulated as impersonal market relationships; yet in the "capitalist sectors" there is no indication, according to Rodinson, that Muslim capitalists have been any more reluctant to exploit people and profits than Christian capitalists. Nor is it unusual that the fourteenth-century genius, the Tunisian Ibn Khaldoun, should write to advise his readers on ways to make profits in trade and land investment, and to counsel them against idle money.

Yet the fact remains that capitalism developed in Europe, and was only introduced from Europe into the Middle East, Ottoman reforms notwithstanding, during the ninteenth and twentieth centuries. Rodinson believes the final evidence for his thesis to be the ease with which capitalism, once introduced, gained a foothold. He is, however, thinking of Turkey and Egypt, not of Afghanistan and Morocco. Nor can he disallow, as one critic points out that, "Islam as a religion could have been used ideologically by a particular ruling group to inhibit certain 'progressive' developments."[8]

Capitalism in Europe required a "free" labor force, the product of the breakdown of feudalism. Nowhere outside of Europe were conditions precisely as they were during the late Middle Ages in Europe. To credit something like capitalism to a particular ideology, ignoring these conditions (which explain the rise of that ideology no less than subsequent economic changes), is unacceptable to Rodinson. He asks, rhetorically, why repeated calls for a Crusade were all unsuccessful after the thirteenth century, when faith was no less than in previous centuries, and answers his own question: "The simple fact was that the religious motives for a Crusade, which were always present, could no longer be integrated in political projects in consonance with the needs of European society in this period."[9] He concludes that if the conditions are right for native capitalism to be able to make and keep profits without lethal competition from foreign capitalism, then the "obstacles constituted by the traditional mentality and the religious and moral bans gradually [fade] away, . . . the demon of capitalist profit invincibly laying hold of ever wider sections . . ."[10]

But of course, these situations did not pertain. Now that the Muslim countries have achieved their independence, when no colonial masters seek to alter the native economy in directions consistent with the economic needs of the home country, if Islamic ideology cannot be charged with anticapitalist bias, then what is the explanation for the contemporary disenchantment among Muslim intellectuals with capitalism as a choice of development strategy? The answer to this probably lies in their recognition of the differences in the histories that Europe and the Middle East have experienced, implying that both ideologies and development strategies cannot be identical. Europe and North America, developed areas with wide strata of affluent, middle-class populations, are easily persuaded by the ideology of capitalism that their situation is not only good but *"just* and in conformity with the nature of things,'' and that their societies cannot benefit from radical alterations. In the Middle East, in contrast, this stratum of society is exceedingly thin; capitalist ideology has ''poor mobilizing power.'' For the intellectuals today who are coming to this conclusion, even Rodinson's defense of their position is vaguely offensive, for he has neglected to challenge the assumption that Weber's association of ''rationality'' and capitalism holds true; some are turning to the suggestion of Marxist critics of capitalism that the ''rationality'' referred to is a kind of Western bourgeois concept, workable for Europe's and America's historical emphasis on individualism and competition, but not necessarily workable everywhere, and certainly not universal. Such ideas appear dangerously radical and are frequently viewed as communist-inspired. But the criticism that has been directed at capitalist thought can just as easily be leveled at Marxist thought, and indeed it has been. Moreover, such views are characteristic only of revolutionary Muslim countries, to which category Egypt no longer can claim to belong, and to which Morocco, Jordan, and obviously the Arabian Peninsula states never have belonged. Egypt's development strategy today is neither capitalist nor socialist but a kind of ''voluntary colonialism'' — the country is a willing dependent of the United States economy. Countries such as Saudi Arabia have never developed socially far enough to create a class structure, and with their oil wealth have neither internal distribution problems nor fear of the world marketplace. Yet, as Islamic states, one might expect that economic rationality would most of all here be sacrificed to religious dogma. The opposite appears to be the case.

Commercial Law and the Sharia

Perhaps the best evidence for the compatibility of Islam and capitalism is in contemporary commercial law and the experiences of foreign firms operating in or transacting business with Arab countries. Despite cultural barriers, Western firms encounter no legal barriers hindering these transactions, even in countries in which the sole source of domestic legal system is the Sharia, such as Saudi Arabia. The reason appears to lie in the fact that the Sharia, as a framework for commercial law, allows for a legislative duality, permitting in international commercial relations the application of foreign law, and even codifying such in the commercial law of the country. Thus the Saudis have adopted a system of commercial courts with provisions derived from the Ottoman commercial and maritime laws (*Tanzimat*), corporation law based on Egyptian and French sources, and numerous provisions and concessions to the foreign oil companies. The only limits applied to the inclusion of these foreign elements is that they may not violate any of the basic principles of Islamic law. That is, they cannot legalize acts forbidden in the Quran, the Sunna, or the ijma, nor can they contradict the intent of these sacred documents. This stipulation has not prevented the Saudi adoption of modern banking laws and tax laws drawn directly from U.S. sources.[11]

The reason underlying the compatibility between the Sharia and modern commercial practices is undoubtedly the common source for the two. The Roman origin of Western laws sets the framework for commercial practices. When Islamic law was in the process of codification, Roman law was paramount throughout the Byzantine world. Islam, from its inception a respecter of the laws of Islamicized areas, incorporated local tradition along with ample portions of Roman law. A basic correspondence between Christian and Muslim world ensued with respect to the legal acknowledgment of contract as the basis for transactional obligations, and the freedom of parties to negotiate and establish the conditions of such contracts, as well as a respect for arbitration of contractual disputes and the acceptance of binding arbitration. Islamic law became highly sophisticated with regard to the law of contracts, and therein lies its flexibility in dealing with modern business affairs.

The Sharia accepts the principle that a contract constitutes the law governing the relationship of the parties to the contract ("*El-adq-shari'at el-muta'quideen*"), providing, of course, that the terms do not violate any principles basic to morality. Thus contracts cannot legalize alcohol, the eating of pork, or riba, although, as Rodinson well understood, the last has, in modern interpretation, permitted the notion of "profit" as a reward for the services performed by money — as long as this does not constitute "unreasonable profit" resulting from greed or exploitation.[12] During the formative period of Islamic jurisprudence, the influence of Greek philosophy through the principle of ijtihad was considerable. Each

Sunni legal tradition seemed to excel in particular expressions of rationality. For example, Abu Hanifa, founder of the Hanafi school, is widely known for his contribution to reasoning, while the development of the science of analogy (arguing from the *qiyas*) to provide decision for religious questions is linked to the Hanbali school. The school of "opinions" (*ray*) found its clearest expression in Maliki legal tradition. Although each Sunni Muslim country has come under the influence of one of these schools of Islamic jurisprudence, all traditions are everywhere considered legitimate. Thus there is nothing to prevent any religious court from adopting an interpretation from Maliki law, with respect to one issue, and using Hanbali law to apply to another. In this way Tunisia has created a path of modernization consistent with Sharia; and in commercial law, the Sharia goes even further, including the possibility of foreign legal interpretations.

Since a contract can include legally binding provisions of foreign origin, as long as they are acceptable to the contracting parties, foreign firms have not found the Sharia an impediment in commercial dealings with Muslim nations. In fact, Islamic law also provides a rational basis for the resolution of commercial disputes. Working from the principle that "the Imam cannot be a judge in his own case," the Sharia permits the establishment of *ad hoc* legal councils whenever governments are parties to disputes and government courts might be involved in a conflict of interests. The grievance councils (*diwan al-mazalim*) are a respected institution, but respect for binding arbitration by international bodies has characterized disputes between Arab countries and foreign oil firms, even when the decisions have gone against these countries. This was the case on several occasions in Saudi Arabia and Abu-Dahbi. Recently, a case between the Libyan *Jamahiriya* and two oil companies ended in a compromise. For, as the late King Faisal said, "We respect the decision of the Court of Arbitration (Geneva) even if it judges against us, for we are bound by that not only according to the rules of the contract but also because our Sharia obliges us to accept arbitration."[13]

Islam and Socialism

To see the Middle East only in terms of the competition between the Western and Eastern blocs has created for Americans a curious dilemma at best; and at worst, it has led to genuine anxiety over the role that Islam will play. On the one hand, according to this scenario, Islam interferes with the modernization of the area, and premodern conditions provide fertile soil for radical ideologies. On the other hand, Islam, a religious faith dogmatically adhered to (as it seems to the readers of *Time* magazine), constitutes a strategic defense against Soviet influence in the area.

The Israeli-Arab conflict has contributed to the polarization of the area, and undoubtedly as a related phenomenon, eminent Middle East scholars have on occasion contributed melodrama rather than clarity and critical analysis of the scenario itself. An example is Bernard Lewis' essay written more than a quarter century ago entitled "Communism and Islam,"[14] in which he posits an affinity between Islam and communism based on a set of similarities including totalitarianism, blind obedience to authority, collectivist tendencies, subjugation of individual freedom, and glorification of conformity, all of which contrast, in his mind, with the values of Judeo-Christian religions. Lewis' methodology of selecting examples sprinkled over the entire Muslim world and fourteen centuries is a classic example of Orientalist obscurantism, in which both Islam and communism are regarded as monolithic systems without history or geography.[15] Often his arguments could be reversed to speak against his assertions. For example, he cites evidence of the "collectivist" tendency in Islam of Sufi movements, but these expressions of popular religion might well be seen as a protest against the overly formalist and insufficiently socially satisfying Islamic orthodoxy. Professor Lewis' reputation as an expert on the Middle East has nevertheless lent this argument a cogency it does not deserve.

It is nevertheless an undeniable fact that as the popularity of socialism has grown in the Muslim countires, the enthusiasm for Western institutions has waned. Not all Western scholars have attributed this to Islam; Malcolm Kerr, for example, who saw trends in the Middle East in the 1960s as largely secular, wrote:

> Liberalism demanded a kind of spontaneous, competitive dynamic equilibrium among social groups, and a kind of in-

dividual moral selfsufficiency, that was precluded by the economic backwardness and class inequality of most Arab countries, and by the unresponsible mentality of the politically conscious classes. . . .[16]

This, of course, does not absolve Islam, for the question of the causes of this economic backwardness and class inequality are still unanswered.

A recent school of neo-Marxist theorists, taking off from the Dependency Theory theses of Andre Gunder Frank and others, has undertaken to write histories which account satisfactorily for the undeveloped world as well as the developed in terms of material causes. A leading scholar of this group, I. Wallerstein, in pursuing the theme that underdevelopment of the Third World was an historical process linked to, and in fact partly responsible for, the development of the industrialized countries, writes that to understand how this happens we must recognize larger-than-state entities as the units of our analysis. Historians have, of course, recognized the existence of empires, but Wallerstein says that characteristic of the modern world is the existence of suprastate systems which do not include political dominance, yet do include dominance of certain states over others, and that it is the rise of capitalism and world markets which has led to such world systems.[17] This inequality, then, that exists in the world, and according to which Muslim countries fall in the category of "underdeveloped" countries, has never depended solely on political subjugation or colonialism. Therefore, the end to colonialism does not solve the problem of underdevelopment, for the world is still encumbered with a system which structures market relations on the principle of power with the "core" (industrial) countries, and weakness with the "peripheral" (non-industrialized) remainder. While the question of unequal terms of trade that is crucial to this theory is debated by economists, the theory is proving increasingly popular among Muslim and non-Muslim leaders in the Third World, for it argues that (1) Middle Eastern intellectuals have been unnecessarily harsh in their criticisms of their own cultures, when the largest portion of the blame for their underdevelopment should have been attributed to economic forces outside their control; and that (2) the possibility of "catch-up" development following Western economic designs is non-existent, thus relieving them of responsibility for their failures since independence. In the on-going debates between "North" and "South" (the U.N. unofficial labels for the rich and poor countries respectively), the arguments of world systems theory are providing the "South" a well-researched theoretical basis for the position that world inequality cannot disappear until the relations of countries to-day structured by world capitalism into a world division of labor and a world-wide class system, can be restructured, transformed by the transformation of the world system itself. It remains to be seen how the use of oil resources as leverage against the power of the in-dustrialized nations can contribute toward this transformation; this is especially unclear, since the division of labor in some oil-rich na-tions is highly uncharacteristic of any of the three worlds — in Kuwait, for example, Kuwaitis are the owners of the means of pro-duction, with all labor contributed exclusively by foreigners; and the Kuwaitis enjoy the highest per capita income in the world. Yet the country cannot be called "developed," nor are there any class ten-sions that do not involve foreigners as one "class." Perhaps registering their vulnerability to Islamic arguments, the oil-rich Arab nations have been generous in their aid to other Muslim coun-tries.

Despite the growing disenchantment with Western institutions, and with Western economic and cultural imperialism, it would be a mistake to see the 1960s popularity of socialism in this area as a decision to emulate the Eastern Bloc out of protest against the West. Socialism has in almost every instance been an outgrowth of na-tionalism, an extension of the liberation struggle to insure that the dominance and exploitation of a former foreign elite will not simply get transferred to an indigenous ruling class following in-dependence. As nationalism was an imported concept, so to many was socialism; its opponents from the middle classes were on occa-sion willing to join forces with Islamic conservatives to resist the tide of this foreign ideology. But others, both secularists and Islamic reformers, found the prospect of a non-foreign socialism enticing. The question became whether socialism was to be the ideology of a kind of secular nationalism, even of revolution, or the ideology of a new, progressive interpretation of Islam. Were claims to an in-dependent socialism based on the unique form of socialism ad-vocated, or simply the uniqueness of the situation to which socialism was to be applied? With many points of view, the results were many and varied.

The relationships and common elements of movements variously labeled "Arab socialism," "Baath Party socialism," "Nasser socialism," "Desturian Socialism," "Islamic Socialism" of the Pakistani People's Party, or the socialism of el-Qaddafi's Libyan jamahiriya challenge the analyst of Middle East affairs to penetrate a protective layer of rhetoric emanating from both advocates and critics, and to search in the underlying substance for identifiable common themes and points of difference. Most important to the present discussion is the question of the relationship of Islam to these several experiments called "socialistic."

Arab nationalism emerged in the Levant during the nineteenth and early twentieth centuries as an anti-Ottoman alliance of Christians and Muslims with different goals: the Muslim nationalists favored returning the Caliphate to Arab hands, while the Christians favored a pan-Arab movement emphasizing pre-Islamic Arab culture, language, and literature. In contrast, the early stirrings of nationalism in Egypt were not anti-Ottoman but anti-British, and not inclined, given Egypt's greater homogeneity, to secular compromises.

Such a secular compromise was the founding of Syria's Baath Party in 1947 by an Orthodox Greek Christian, Michel Aflaq, and a Sunni Muslim, Salaheddine al-Bitar, two high-school teachers dedicated to Arab unity, independence from European hegemony, a secular socialist program and ideology aimed at national integrity, a renaissance of Arab spirit, and a constitutional government based on the concept of parliamentary democracy. Though a current issue of the N.Y. *Times* refers to the Syrian Baath ideology as "radical," it was in fact less revolutionary than reformist, and the term "socialism" was used sparingly.

As one of many, and a minority party, the Baath supported union with Nasser's Egypt in 1959, an experiment in "Arab unity" which lasted exactly two years.

Nasser's move toward socialism was gradual, and if influenced by the pan-Arab objectives of the Baath leaders, less explicity secular. The leaders of a 1952 Egyptian *coup d'etat* which overthrew the pro-British monarch, Nasser and his "Free Officers" were faced with ruling Egypt, the need for a program to meet the demands of a situation everyone took to be a revolution, and the need for an ideology to suit that program. The last was only forthcoming with the 1962 National Charter, which explicitly defined Egypt's experiment as socialist. By then, Nasser had been forced, through a combination of economic needs (insufficient investment capital) and international politics (the nationalization of the Suez canal, invasion by Israeli, British, and French forces), into the nationalization of large firms, banks, insurance companies, and major industries — in short, into creating a public-sector-dominated economy which capitalists referred to as socialist, and Marxists referred to as "state capitalism."

Nasser was no ideologue. Influenced by Nehru, whom he met at Bandung, Nasser was committed to development and to social justice, and appeared to favor a secular solution to both, based on co-operative socialism. The aims of the revolution, he insisted, were compatible with the principles of Islam:

> The essence of all religion is the assertion of Man's right to dignity and freedom. The very doctrine of reward and punishment is based on the concept of equality of opportunity for everyman before God . . . for the will to be free, the person must be free. True religion cannot tolerate a restrictive system of class distinction, by virtue of which the majority inherit the terrestrial punishment of poverty, ignorance and disease, while a small minority monopolizes the reward of all prosperity[18]

The Ikhwan al-Muslimin (Muslim Brotherhood) were far from satisfied with the regime's position. Although they had supported the anit-imperialist struggle, which recognized only the community of believers (*umma*), they opposed the very notion of nationalism as foreign and anti-Islam. Nasser's brand of nationalism was too secular and too receptive to foreign ideas. The ideas they found offensive were more likely to be progressive ideas about women, not about workers. The ideas of Hasan al-Banna, their founding leader, were fairly progressive with respect to workers.

Most Arab and Western writers appear to have regarded Nasser's socialism as secular. Thus Professor Sharabi refers to it as a continuation of Attaturk's secular development:

> The "socialist" revolution which now arose first in Egypt and Syria, and later in Algeria and Iraq, was the culmination of the movement of secular modernization that had its roots in the late nineteenth century. It had embarked upon a road which inevitably divorced Arab society from the remnants of its religious past. The attitude of uncompromising reformism which characterized the Kemalist "revolution" in Turkey a few decades earlier was fully taken up by the Arab revolutionaries of the mid-twentieth century.[19]

Western writers saw Nasser's attempts to gain Islamic legitimacy for his revolution as "lip service" and expedient. Masannat writes:

> They [Nasser] have used the non-ritualistic Muslim religion as a vehicle to provide the necessary force for the modernization and transformation lying ahead. Thus Nasser of Egypt, unlike Mustafa Kemal of Turkey, who established the principle of separation of church and state in his nation and kept education and law free from religious domination, paid lip service to Islamic institutions, heritages, myths, and symbols in the hopes of establishing his democratic socialistic state which is in practice no more than an authoritarian welfare state. Furthermore, while Kemal viewed Turkey as a "secular" state, Nasser explicitly recognized Islam as the religion of the state. However . . . Mustafa Kemal became the guiding and inspiring leader to Gamal Abdel Nasser, who views himself as the Attaturk of Egypt.[20]

A Christian Arab critic challenges the claim that Egyptian socialism is justified on religious grounds, thus supporting the arguments of the Ikhwan:

> On two cardinal issues, then, Islam can safely be said to be at variance with the official ideology of the Egyptian regime. Insofar as it is borrowing from the secular, materialistic West, Arab socialism is an alien intrusion into the Islamic policy and society, and the attempt to present Islam now as "democracy," now as "socialism" amounts to nothing less than making a travesty of its fundamental principles. Arab nationalism — the other principal component of Nasserism — is likewise an aberration, a negation of the universal character of Islam and a manifestation of pagan jahiliyya.[21]

Nasser's defense against such accusations was a reiteration of the common goals of Islam and his revolution. Reaction, he said, was always ready to monopolize the good things of the earth, and in the past did so by harnessing religion to the service of its own greed; but the true message of all religions is a call to progress. In general, Nasser appears to have left to others the problem of Islamic legitimacy, taking pains rather that Egyptian socialism not be identified with the Marxist variety. His official spokesman, Mohammad Haykal, summarized the ways in which Nasser's Arab socialism contrasts with Marxist programs. According to Haykal,[22] and presumably Nasser, Nasser's socialism and communism differ in their views on class and class struggle, the ownership of property legitimately obtained, the treatment of exploiters, and the compensation for property confiscated by the government. In all these, the Arab variety of socialism is regarded as the more humane, but Islamic morality is not invoked.

In social theory, Haykal continues, Arab socialism differs from communism by regarding the individual as the basis of the social structure and the state a mere tool for attaining justice for the individual. Moreover, the Arab socialist state refuses to sacrifice present generations for the sake of future ones; it is free from dogma and willing to consider foreign ideas. Finally, Haykal notes, the Arab socialist state is built, not on the leadership of a single political party, but on the participation of the entire nation.

The Nasser regime, by not declaring itself secularist, and Nasser himself, by invariably opening his speeches with quotes from the Quran, kept alive the ambiguity with respect to the Islamic character of Egyptian socialism. An unsolicited contribution to this ambiguity was the conclusion by the head of the Ikhwan in Syria, and the author of a treatise on Islamic socialism that the Nasser program seemed compatible with Islamic socialism. The ambiguity was probably inevitable. Malcolm Kerr recognized this in every attempt to contrast Arab socialism with the scientific socialism of Marx. To Kerr, the differences clearly evoke the Islamic basis of the "reality of the Arabs" — Islam's rejection of materialist history, and class struggle, and its respect for private property and commerce. He sees the problem in both nationalism and socialism, insofar as they are defined as "Arab" without explicitly basing their ideologies on Islam:

> Nationalism has established itself as a vital force in the Arab world precisely because it has avoided a confrontation with religion. It has blurred in the popular mind, and even in many educated minds the difference between the Islamic *umma* (community) and the Arab *umma* (nation), capitalizing instead on the inextricable historical relations between the two, by virtue of which each is in some sense a vital part of the other. . . . Contradictions arise to the surface only when nationalists consider modern principles of political and social action. . . .[23]

Christian nationalists have been forced to acknowledge that among the symbols of an emergent Arab nationalism, none was more closely bound to the high points of Arab history than Islam. Yet secularism has appeared the only viable strategy in areas, such as Syria, that not only included large Christian populations but diverse Muslim ones as well (Alawite, Shiite, Druze), not to mention ethnic plurality (Kurds, etc.). The situation remains unresolved today, exacerbated by the instability in Lebanon, where genuine class struggle continues to be remolded into confessional hostilities exaggerated by outside intervention by Syrians and Israelis, and a large resident Palestinian population of refugees. "Arab" here has no unitary meaning; but "Muslim" and "Christian" also have virtually none. Even the unity of political factions has degenerated into interfamily strife.

The difficulty in identifying the ideology of the Nasser regime is because it was never clear, according to Egyptian Marxists. One Marxist supporter of the regime, Muhammed Awda, summarizes the eclectic approach of the Free Officers who, after the 1952 *coup d'etat,* persuaded themselves that the failure of the Wafd Party (Nationalists) to mobilize the nation and furnish direction to the revolution did not eliminate nationalism as an ideological force. Nor did the failure of the Communist Party and the socialists to find a way of relating their social theories to the realities of the Egyptian masses necessarily eliminate these as potential sources for an Egyptian revolutionary ideology. Finally, the failure of the Ikhwan to seize leadership did not eliminate Islam as a source. Thus the regime "refrained from rejecting any of the ideologies prevalent in Egypt at the time; indeed it flirted with all of them, trying to preserve something of each, without committing itself to any of them."[24]

Egypt under Nasser never succeeded in defining an ideology for development that was unambiguously socialist and either unambiguously secular or unambiguously Islamic. Rather, it produced the National Charter of 1962, sufficiently ambiguous for Egyptians of many persuasions to offer it support without having to compromise any of their beliefs. Under Sadat, the rhetoric of socialism has disappeared as Egypt's economy moves steadily to the right. Without Nasser and with his policies discredited, the debate has apparently permanently polarized, thanks to the combined efforts of fundamentalist and traditionalist sheikhs at Al Azhar, into a contest between Islam and Marxism, a contest in which Marxism has not a ghost of a chance. Islam and authenticity are pitted against atheism and alien ideology. Advocates of progressive reform chastise the religious establishment and the people for listening to the religious establishment, while liberal Marxists willingly assign some of the blame to those orthodox Marxists who play into the hands of fundamentalist polarization by reiterating Marx's opinion that religion is merely an opiate of the people. Polarization has its uses: both sides appear unreasonable, so reasonable people move toward the center. Perhaps President Sadat benefits from the arrangement. But many are exasperated and passionately so, as this contribution to a leftist journal, allowed to publish until 1976, indicates:

> It is both irrational and anti-Islam that a society could exist where 90% of the people are utterly poor and 10% are quite rich . . . [yet these critics] are neither calling for social equality and justice nor do they give up their money to people who need. . . . Does it satisfy your religious sensitivities that in Cairo there are 100,000 private cars serving about 200,000 people, and about 1,000 busses serving about 3 million who spend their lives standing by empty bus stops while airconditioned limousines with the family dog pass them by?[25]

During Nasser's leadership, critics from the left, noting the harshness with which he treated communists, questioned whether any state could be called socialist which lacked leaders who were socialists in their ideology. Such was the situation in the 1960s. Today, while the economy of Egypt makes an upheaval at least possible, while most intellectuals identify with the left and are critical of the new policies of "Open Door" and the Americanization of Egypt, there appears little chance that opposition to the government will be directed either by the secularist left or by the progressive Islamic group, all of whom are safely isolated from the masses. Fundamentalist student movements are today the most daringly outspoken critics of the regime and its growing dependency on America and Americans.

In Algeria, where Marxism has had a far greater influence on revolutionary ideology and the development of a socialist strategy, the role of Islam is still ambiguous, and the official position of the state is one which can only be described as "when in doubt, trill"! Gordon relates this to the "identity crisis" of Algerians, and the fact that in the independence struggle the nation faced an enemy which was European and Christian, making almost inevitable the employment of symbols of resistance drawn from Islam. Gordon sees the debate over the aims of the revolution in bipolar terms (admittedly a simplification) in which:

For the Marxist modernist, Castro and Tito are closer as "brothers" in [the search for equality with the developed nations] than is Nasser. Lip-service might be paid to Algeria's Islamic character, and gratitude expressed for the role of religion in preserving the "national personality" under colonialism, and in serving as a motor-force during the Revolution. With independence, however, religion is to be subordinated to a "scientific" reconstruction of society.

The second pole, the Islamist, is the point of view which sees the Revolution as essentially a struggle to restore and reform a suppressed and consequently perverted religious tradition, and to protect it from alien and atheistic ideologies, in short from "pieds rouges" as it once needed protection from the "pieds noirs."[26]

The strength of the Islamic elements is demonstrated in the reformist ulema opposition to the nationalization of the small holdings under Algerian Muslim peasant ownership at the time that those rich, large holdings vacated by the *pieds noirs* were nationalized and "socialized" under a system of *autogestion* (self-management by the workers). Of course, not all of the Islamic reformers felt that socialism and Islam were incompatible. Modernist-progressives advocated the interpretation of Islam as essentially socialist, a "religion of the poor against the rich." Yet polarization into a conflict between "Muhammad's socialism" and "Marx's socialism," as in the Egyptian debates, has occurred. Conflicting ideological positions have fought to dominate Algeria's revolutionary direction and its strategy for development: on the one hand, the highly decentralized "self-management" form of production, and on the other, a highly centralized "state socialism." The former was a phenomenon which "happened" with the French pull-out, rather than being imposed by the government. Politically it represents a radical statement about the stage of revolution entered into, a stage apparently well in advance of any ideological preparation by workers themselves. The only effective organization with independence was the state in the hands of an educated political elite. Even though state socialism ran the risk that ". . . with state-run enterprises coming to the fore, with state planning, and with a state monopolizing the public interest, government would become the private property of bourgeois nationalists and the state bourgeoisie,"[27] the self-management experiment was virtually dismantled by 1967. Curiously, this debate over socialist strategy could not remain apart from the secular-religious debate which somehow assimilated it. Eventually the notion of autogestion was perceived as Soviet (!) and denounced as foreign, more damning to Islamic socialists than the nationalization of property. Thus a radical form of socialist organization in Algeria which would have removed the question of class struggle as a bone of contention between "Muhammad's socialists" and "Marx's socialists" was discontinued under the pressure of Islam-related arguments. At the same time, the editor of the official journal of the UGTA (General Union of Algerian Workers) was jailed for permitting the publication of a letter praising Algeria's Islamic-Arabic socialism because it rejected class struggle and respected private property![28]

Two obviously contradictory positions regarding Islam continue to coexist in Algeria. In one, "Islam's significance is derived from socialism and not the other way around," according to the (mainly) Marxist advocates of "scientific socialism" who are secularist in their separation of "church and state." In the second, socialism is derived from Islamic sources, and provides the basis of an Algerian identity and legitimacy for its revolution and development strategies. While contradictory, both of the ideas seem indispensable. Without faith as cement, the stresses and strains of modernization may prove lethal. The state, however, can only operate in the area of technical decisions by adopting a wholly secular position. Algeria is thus operated as a two-sector society, with the government carefully avoiding any confrontation between the two. One, the technical-scientific world of development, is carefully focused on industrializing the country without creating any dependency on foreign powers. The other, the Islamic world of "moral rearmament," rules over the social organization of society. By an implicit agreement between the Marxist planners and the religious establishment "The religious ideology holds sway over the family but allows Marxism a free hand in everything that concerns the transition to socialism. Marxism returns the compliment and avoids meddling with the family unit, and more broadly speaking, with matters that concern the status of women."[29] Thus, the Arab socialism of

Algeria, though economically progressive, remains socially traditional. Women who gained a kind of equality during the Revolution as the partners of their men in guerilla warfare have reverted to a subordinate position which Egyptian women, not to mention the liberated women of Tunisia, would find unacceptable.

The contrast between Tunisia and Algeria is interesting. Tunisia's development strategy since independence, as guided by Bourguiba and the "socialism" of the Desturian Party, has rather reversed the emphasis of Algeria's: the legitimacy of the Tunisian program was based, not on the juggling act of Algeria's leaders who were able to "turn to socialism with the Koran in one hand and *Das Kapital* in the other,"[30] but by "rationalizing" Islamic sources of legitimacy. Thus it was possible for social reforms to be made in the name of Islam, by carefully selecting a combination of Maliki, Hanbali, and Hanafi legal traditions. An interpretation of the Prophet's stricture that a man cannot have more than one wife unless he can provide each equal treatment was judged to be tantamount to disapproval of polygyny on the argument that equal treatment is simply impossible; and the state outlawed polygyny. Rulings on the appropriateness of fasting during *Ramadan* for certain workers were liberalized as well. Divorce laws were modernized to improve women's position.

At the same time, the Tunisian version of "socialism" bears no resemblance to Marx's. Private property is not only a legal right, but the government has engaged in large-scale decollectivization programs, alloting former state lands, collectively operated for a period by resettled populations from the south, to family units as private holdings in a kind of reverse-twist land reform. In Tunisia, modernism triumphs.

A socialist program, this time clearly legitimized in the name of Islam, was that of Pakistan's late head of government, Ali Bhutto, recently executed on charges of murdering an opponent. Bhutto's Pakistan People's Party was a collection of diverse elements without any ideological homogeneity. Bhutto himself was the product of a wealthy landowning aristocratic family and was educated in Britain and the United States.[31] Convinced that Pakistan's government under Ayub Khan (in which he had held a cabinet post) was corrupt, Bhutto was instrumental in the unified opposition and protests that led to Ayub's resignation and to his own rise to power. The newly formed P.P.P. took the position that Pakistani development had proceeded at the cost of "massive plundering of the economy by private entrepreneurs,"[32] often financed with public funds, and aided by a permissive government attitude toward fraud, and an oppressive one toward labor unions. Only socialism could cure Pakistan. A realist, Bhutto also recognized that a state founded on the principle of Muslim nationalism could never dissociate Islam from its national heritage. The problem was to sell socialism as a system not antithetical to religious values. The time was ripe, since the popularity of socialism as a protest ideology in the context of maldistributed wealth had reached a high point in the 1960s.

Bhutto's "Islamic socialism" was, however, more rhetoric than ideology. Land reform failed to satisfy true socialists; and the government's socialist ideology became more a means of justifying its actions than a guide for action. Eventually, Pakistan's socialism was reduced to little more than slogans. Thus, it justified private property as consistent with Pakistan's version of Islamic socialism; but it equally justified the confiscation of property by the government on "socialist" grounds.[33]

While both socialism and Islam in the mouths of politicians suffer from charges of insincerity, a few scholarly proponents of a progressive interpretation of Islam continue to argue the compatibility of socialism and reformed Islam. Among their predecessors they claim one of the most influential Islamic reformers of the late nineteenth century, Jamal al-Din al-Afghani (1838-1897), whose use of the term *ishtirakiyya* (socialism) may be the earliest recorded.[34] Al-Afghani's view of *ishtirakiyyat al-Islam* (Islamic socialism) was that it owed nothing to Western socialist doctrines, with which he claimed familiarity. It resulted rather from Islam's adoption of a pre-Islamic emphasis on sharing among Bedouins, with the result that the Islamic state came to have carefully built-in welfare stipulations of responsibilities for the rich toward the poor, the warrior toward the nonwarrior, and so forth. This reconstruction of a tribal "socialism" brings to mind Marx's need to demonstrate, by reconstructing a stage of early communism, that communism, if given a chance, works.

The problem Islam confronted, al-Afghani reasoned, was one of preserving the unity and solidarity of an egalitarian society, once there were not just wealth differences, but the arrogant display of wealth in the face of contrasting misery, a situation the enlightened caliphs were supposed to have avoided up until the "self-indulgent Umayyads."

The differences we refer to might be described in terms of the distinction between *modernization* and *development*. The oil-rich and sparsely populated desert nations of the Arabian Peninsula (Libya with its Mediterranean heritage has chosen a different path) with their tribal kingdoms have opted for modernization, for buying a prefab technology and the necessary expertise to assemble it. Their world image is less important than is the weight they carry in the world's financial markets; internally, modernization is technical but not social, since the productive forces of the societies are almost exclusively imported workers. Such societies are "modernizing" rapidly in the sense of material comforts, but "developing" very slowly, if at all, with few pressures for either social change (other than through the foreign education of the young men), or genuine capitalist organization. The Sharia accommodates the premodern social system and modern commercial needs equally well. The temptation of these wealthy landlords to imitate their employees is slight.

Very different are those populous Muslim nations, some with few resources, that have lived through both the glories of early civilizations and the humiliations of colonialism and dependency. Their major need today is a national strategy for *development,* not just for modernization; in fact, the "modernization" they underwent during their colonial period is now part of their problem, rather than a contributing solution to the problem. These countries have the class structures of the underdeveloped world affected by, but not corrected by, revolutions of one sort or another. The choice of development strategy for these Muslim nations is more complex. Intertwined with what to the Western mind is a set of pragmatic considerations (targets for GDP, etc.) are questions of ideology. The choice of an ideology is complicated, because this ideology must be capable of serving the pragmatic development strategies and at the same time provide legitimacy for a new identity to replace the counterproductive self-image that generations of humiliating dependency left as a legacy.

It is easy for the Egyptian wit to produce parodies of the Americanized Arab returning to his country to pretend he no longer knows how to behave as an Arab, and becoming ridiculous in this counterfeit role. It is more difficult to formulate a workable identity which is sufficiently "modern" for today's intellectuals to wear with pride. Given the close linkage between the identity problem and development, it is perhaps understandable why it grows increasingly difficult to write a scenario for an independent development in the Muslim world that ignores Islam. Professor Sharabi's obituary for Islam as an influence on Middle East society now appears premature.[39] Two possibilities occur: the leadership will remain as secular as it seemed to be in the 1960s, but the mobilization of the masses will require an Islamic legitimacy for the leadership; or the intellectuals will discover that, among the possible identities they can forge for themselves, "being Muslim" is inescapable: for even the non-believer in Islam, Islam is the "civilization of reference." It corresponds not to Christianity, but to "Christendom." This inevitable Islamic identity is inescapable even for Christian Arabs, unless they wish to relinquish their Arabness. It feeds the suspicion that the Soviet path to development requires commitments that are both foreign and atheist. And yet, there is the growing conviction that the "liberal democracy" of the West is highly selective. Western principles of human rights do not seem to apply, for example, to Palestinians. Thus, despite the many failures of the Soviets to establish close relationships with the Arab Middle East, the United States is seen increasingly not as a benefactor, but as the power behind the Zionist-colonialist intrusion. The 1967 "June War" recalled visions of Arab ignominy in the face of European imperialism. For the political left, Israel represents a colonial outpost of American imperialism, today joined by Egypt. The political left has usually been at odds with the religious establishment. Today, common grounds of agreement rather suggest an entente. In addition to matters such as population control and wealth redistribution, the areas of agreement include rejection of the assumption that only two paths to development exist — those sponsored by the Western-capitalist or the Eastern-socialist blocs. Advocates of an Islamic path run the gamut from fundamentalist to modernist, from conservative to progressive. Yet the representatives of each of these categories can agree on one general position: despite their different evaluations of the relative merits of the capitalist Western bloc and the socialist Eastern bloc formulas for development, they agree that there is a superior third way, and that way is Islamic.

Thus, in a pamphlet published by the American Enterprise Institute, Sheikh Abdul-Rauf explains why a Muslim society should not copy either Western capitalism or Western socialism:

> Capitalism idolizes the individual, regards his personal freedom as a sacred and precious gift, trusts him with the task of maximizing production, and forbids state interference in the entrepreneur's initiative . . . socialism [insists] on the state control of

the . . . means of production . . . usurps the individual's liberty
of economic action, denies him the chance to exercise his initiative, kills his incentive to work hard for greater personal gain,
and deprives him of much of his dignity. While capitalism is a
decentralized system that provides the individual with unlimited
room for dynamism, imaginative ambition, inventiveness, and
improvement, socialism is a centralized system that is to a great
degree static. The state administers the . . . means of production
and controls the will of the masses. Yet capitalistic ideas breed
selfishness, cruel individualism, and greed and are bound to
create a climate of loneliness and isolation. The atmosphere of
severe competitiveness is bound to lead to deep tension and
depression, resulting in domestic instability, criminality, corruption on a large scale, and a deep fear of insecurity since there can
be no limit to selfish ambitions. Unbridled socialism, on the other
hand, is capricious, transgressive, and dehumanizing and has also
led to widespread corruption and nepotism. Socialism owes its
rise to envy, jealousy, and dissatisfaction; in its extreme form it
therefore calls for class struggle and the elimination of the van-
quished class. The ideal of both systems is simply materialistic,
with little or no concern for the spiritual needs of the
individual. . . .[40]

Intellectuals within as well as outside the religious establishment
agree that the civilizations of the West suffer from severe defects;
their material prosperity is at the cost of human values; and each of
these civilizations dominating the world today is a kind of Cyclops
— able to see with only one eye, and therefore lacking perspective.
One is an advanced technological society, advanced politically
(liberal democracy) but socially backward, with severe deficiencies
in the realm of social justice, and impoverished spiritually and
ethically. The other has also achieved admirable advances in industrial technology, and in addition is socially enlightened; but it is
politically backward (there is a deficiency in democratic freedoms),
and it is also spiritually and ethically impoverished. Any Third Path
should be instructed by useful ideas of these civilizations, but it
must in addition provide positive solutions to replace their defective
aspects. Advocates of reformed Islam claim that this Third Path
should be an Islamic one. They acknowledge that the problem is
double-barreled. It includes both the internal problem of development of infrastructure, industrialization, public health, education,

wealth distribution, *and* the external problem of liberation from exploitation by the developed industrial countries and the attainment of equal partnership of nations through some new system of global justice.

There are, of course, obstacles in the way of effecting the transformations necessary for this development. But the internal obstacles of the Muslim nations are, according to these advocates, considerably less than elsewhere in the Third World. Consider, writes al-Sadek al-Mahdi, the great innovators of Western civilization: Immanuel Kant, preaching the value of human intellect; Karl Marx, teaching the importance of history to an understanding of social justice; Sigmund Freud, insisting that the key to an understanding of human behavior lay in the recognition of the power of elemental sexual urges. All were forced to convince a society in which the human intellect, social justice, and basic instincts were considered dangerous to society. Islam is the unique example of a world religion which positively values the human intellect, social justice, and basic biological drives such as sex, placing each in a system with reasonable limits. A truly Islamic society would not have needed Kant, Marx, or Freud to make these values acceptable.[41]

Consider, too, the divisive ideologies that underlie caste and class divisions. Ethnic divisions and religious divisions exist in the Muslim world, but Islam is uniquely suited to resolving these, say its advocates. Only Islam, they believe, can contribute to societal revitalization at the same time that it legitimizes plans for modernization.

Islam, moreover, does not need to sacrifice spiritualism to be compatible with these humanist values. It is founded on divinely inspired insight acquired through a genuine miracle: the Quran is the written word of God revealed to an illiterate man, who became not only the advocate of a new religion but the founder of a new state, a rare combination of prophet and statesman.

Although the intellectualist tradition of Islam, once so powerful, has over the past few centuries been obscured by dogma, the last defense of a beaten civilization, it is vital and alive at the core, say the reformers — fundamentalists and modernists alike. The true tradition of Islam urges maximum use of all kinds of knowledge: spiritual, intellectual, and empirical. As for the last, one need cite only the Sufi directive: "As you walk on earth, look around you. Every new piece of knowledge is proof of the existence of God."

Reason is not the enemy of faith, as has been so often said by secularists. It is reason that has translated the intent of God's message to the Prophet into workable ethical and legal prescriptions. "Nobody's belief is complete until he wants for his brother that which he wants for himself" provides an ethical basis for social justice stronger than the mere obligation of almsgiving.

The altruist in the Islamic society is admired, not ridiculed as "irrational," nor suspected as a demagogue.

Perhaps the most important aspect claimed for Islam by its advocates, in the context of development needs, is its capacity to emphasize spiritual, external, and universalistic phenomena, and thus permit Muslims to be members of the faith in an uncompromising way, and at the same time "progressive" in the social sense. These advocates insist that other religions either sacrifice spirituality in the interests of rational-progressive change; or else they insist on spirituality at the cost of reactionary positions toward change.

Advocates find in the above assumptions about their religion a basis for intellectual as well as moral rearmament, through which they should be able to resist the temptation to imitate either Western bloc or Eastern bloc solutions to the problems of development, and by resisting, contribute not only to their own civilization's development, but to the world's. They agree that they will provide a source for a Third World independent development, attractive even to non-Muslims because it offers a global system based on justice for all nations.

In promoting this Third Path, the Arab nations have a unique role, by virtue of the special relationship between their national history and Islam, by virtue of the oil resources available to them, and finally, by virtue of their identification with the international injustices culminating in the Zionist violation of Palestine. But while a secular Arab renaissance is apparently impossible, some say it will be equally impossible for any Arab renaissance to take place without an achieved harmony with the other Muslim peoples — Turks, Persians, Africans — who constitute natural allies in the global struggle. If the world today is characterized by unequal distribution of wealth and power, there is little likelihood of a more equitable distribution from a non-Islamic source without struggle. The spread of Islam could help tip the balance; but the political use of resources such as oil to neutralize the imbalance of power is more frequently regarded as a duty, whether or not it is linked with *jihad*.

The above composite scenario is one which emphasizes not so much an Islamic system drawn exclusively from Quranic and Sunna sources (as, for example, the Ikhwan al-Muslimin insists on) as one which in its technical aspects makes selective use of the advances of the Western world (including the Eastern bloc) but which imbues this material equipment of civilization with the spiritual inspiration of "the East." Reduced to this level, it resembles the stereotyped distinction separating the two halves of the world (in which Japan constitutes a distinct anomaly) — a materialist West, a spiritual East. But the Arab versions claim a more historically specific scenario: Islam isn't just an Oriental religion, it is unique. It is the only one that can bridge these worlds, and in the process, it also appears to bridge the "two cultures" which C.P. Snow wrote about a couple of decades ago, the "scientific" culture and the "humanist" culture.

The advocates of an Islamic solution to the development of the Third World who espouse the modernist approach accept scientific principles as a necessary, but insufficient, basis for developing a modern society.

It is hard to counter their argument that major defects exist in the two world-systems, even while protesting that their picture of the societies in the "Two Worlds" are caricatures; for they are accurate caricatures, putting in relief the good with the bad and leaving out the ho-hum aspects in which all world societies are coming to resemble one another.

It is healthy to see how one's society and culture appear in the eyes of outsiders. In the U.S. and in the U.S.S.R. citizens who wish to feel comfortable with their respective systems can assure themselves of their right choices in being born Americans or Russians by comparing the idealized version of their own system with the observed version of the other's. A third party, disaffected by both, can be objective, if not necessarily about his criteria, at least in his observations.

We in this country do not believe that ours is a society of technology at the cost of human exploitation. We believe we have a system of laws, and therefore of justice. What we seldom consider is that our society is the product of a certain history, and that our way of valuing has come about as the precipitate of historical events more than as a result of detached human reflections. We believe that our civilization has achieved more in the interests of human rights than the rest of the world. We are suspicious of the role of a state, other than in co-ordinating that which individuals do. We believe it should interfere only to minimize the hardships of the losers in our competitive system. This is to satisfy our humanitarian feelings, the source of which is religion rather than Adam Smith. We are thus often forced to choose between morality and rationality, since these come to us from different traditions that have coexisted but never coalesced. Islam promises a happy marriage of morality and rationality. Is this achievable only in the utopian society, or is there a practical possibility that such a system could work?

The most provocative experiment today seems to us to be not the Iranian revolution, which still must resolve many problems that prevent Iran from behaving as a state, the only unity deriving at the moment from hatred of the United States. The most interesting case is that of Libya. Are we here looking at a private experiment in whimsey, a preview of the progressive state of the twenty-first century, or what? What precisely is the Islamic contribution to this radical form of socialist democracy?

In attempting to make sense of the Libyan experiment, one confronts a major difficulty: the "evidence" is limited to two sorts of documentation: on one hand, the official and therefore idealized versions of el-Qaddafi's Jamahiriya, along with statistics on the material development of the country; and on the other, the equally propagandistic, if unofficial, media reports on Libya, with the uninformed references to dictatorship and Islamic fundamentalism. That el-Qaddafi is a devout Muslim can be granted. The relevance of Islam in the development of a revolutionary approach to restructuring society and economy is less clear.

What precisely is the *Green Book,* authored by Muaamar el-Qaddafi?[42] It is not a little book of inspirational messages as was the *Thoughts of Mao Tse-tung,* although its title indicates an awareness of the inevitability of comparison with the "little red book" that figured so prominently in China's cultural revolution. Nor is the *Green Book* the culmination of a life career of study, as is the case with *Das Kapital*; in fact, the economic part of the *Green Book,* in the English translation, is a mere 31 pages! In a sense, it is to be compared with the Communist Manifesto, though its rhetoric is noninflammatory. Actually, it goes into no detail at all, provides no definitions of such key terms as "need", "production", or "social justice." It avoids references to both Quranic sources and Marxist ones, although inspired by both. While Marxist jargon is conspicuous by its absence, it seems to us that references to "natural" systems of economic exchange, implying ones in which producers have control over the use, distribution, and consumption of their products, are more likely to be rooted in Marx than Muhammad. It cannot be called a blueprint for revolution; it offers no instructions on *how* the new society is to be achieved, other than through every individual's accepting the responsibility of active participation in the process of government by the people. Much of the modernizing process appears to be seen by el-Qaddafi as straightforward technical solutions to technical problems, unlike, say, Mao's "Great Leap" program in which ideology and organization were expected to make up for lack of expertise and technical backwardness. The *Green Book* is a brief outline in slogan form, reminiscent of army manuals, a vision according to government-sanctioned spokesmen, the vision of a generation of young revolutionaries who became army officers, who engineered the coup of 1969, and who chose el-Qaddafi as their leader.

Nonetheless, it seems apt to compare the *Green Book* with the Communist Manifesto. El-Qaddafi presents his "economic solution" (Part II) as a proposed new step forward in history's struggle to "rationalize" (not his term) production relations. As Marx and Engels presented communism in the context of a dialetical theory of history, as a solution to the internal contradictions of capitalism, so el-Qaddafi takes a kind of Hegelian world-system view, regards Marxism as antithesis to capitalism's thesis, and draws the conclusion that the new synthesis will be according to his vision. The Libyan Jamahiriya with its socialist economy will prevail as the vanguard of a Third World development strategy independent of the Two Worlds. This is, admittedly, to read a great deal between the lines of a brief document which only uses the phrase "dialectical solution" once. Yet it is in keeping with el-Qaddafi's use of "Third Universal Theory." Many have interpreted the universality of el-Qaddafi's principle to be Islam. To a mystic like el-Qaddafi, a dialectical process and an omnipotent being are possibly not contradictory, nor are processes and forces of inevitable change and the changeless message of God which is timeless and valid everywhere.

The economics of the *Green Book* are clearly socialist, if not necessarily clear to a socialist. The message is primitive: needs create production; participation in production creates rights to consume, yet these are limited by needs, so that the capacity to consume beyond needs — or even to save beyond needs, for this is equivalent to the right to future consumption — is deemed to occur only at another's expense and thus is not allowed. The rationale is not totally clear, but might be the following: if a society's production is targeted to meet needs, and this target is achieved, then only unequal distribution which rewards one at the cost of exploiting another (interfering with his needs) can increase any individual's wealth. It is interesting that in our capitalist world, some writers are pointing to a fast-approaching zero-sum society. Perhaps Colonel el-Qaddafi has anticipated them by assuming this condition.

Wage-work in the new society must give way to partnerships of producers and "profit-sharing," although the term "profit" will also disappear when socialism replaces capitalist enterprise. At least, it will disappear as an incentive. If the *Green Book's* radical political message is the total rejection of representative government in favor of rule by all the people through a hierarchy of committees and a virtual absence of formal government, then the radical economic message is that a wage system is tantamount to slavery — or charity. Both are evils. Wage-work is evil because the worker lacks control over his product and its disposal. To regard charity as a social evil is presumably one of those radical ideas which convince the conservative Muslims that el-Qaddafi's Islam is heretical.

Only socialism and a genuine people's ownership of the means of production can eliminate the wage system, for then the workers work for themselves and presumably have a voice in determining their conditions.

The rewards of production are to be limited to those who participate in it, and will not be influenced by differences in skills, experience, stamina, or efficiency. Any surplus value produced in excess of the needs of the producers belongs to all the people. Presumably the people collectively make decisions on the use, investment, or consumption of this surplus product. One way is indicated for its dispensation: those who contribute to the *collective* welfare by efforts beyond their productive role, which is rewarded according to their needs, may receive additional rewards. Thus a basis for differential rewards other than that established on different needs is offered; and here, perhaps, is a continuing basis for work incentive beyond the level of needs satisfaction. But can *altruism* be rewarded without suffering its destruction?

The system does not make all rights to consume contingent on production. Rather, it proposes that to be rewarded from production enterprise one must be a *contributor* to the production. Needs alone determine the consumption level, and should in certain cases by fulfilled by the government (now, presumably, by the Jamahiriya-designated agents). On the principle that "Man's freedom is lacking if somebody else controls what he needs," houses, vehicles, tractors, etc. are dispensed to those who establish a need for them. No one can claim the need for a house unless he owns none and is living in another's house. In operation, Libyans have been granted ownership of the houses they inhabited, or the apartments. ("Dwelling" rather than "house" should perhaps have been promised, but the *Green Book* stipulates "house," and indeed, one-family houses have been constructed in huge numbers.)

No one who is not a producer deserves any income from production, but "producer" covers all who contribute to production: workers, managers, suppliers of raw materials and tools (of course the public will be the supplier in many cases). What determines the distribution of rewards from production? According to the *Green Book,* each *factor of production* is as essential to production as every other factor of production; thus all factors share an equal part of the value produced. According to an illustration given, in factory production a third of the revenues will go to the factory, another third to the supplier of capital (machines), and a final third to the "producers" (wages and salaries). So if the factory and its machines are publicly owned, the "people" collectively will receive two-thirds of a factory's revenues. This formula does not obviously suggest a particular source, whether capitalist, socialist, or Quranic.

How Islamic is the Libyan Jamahiriya? Compared to the programs put forth by the authors of the versions of Islamic socialism referred to above, the Libyan form seems not to claim, even implicitly, an exclusive Islamic legitimacy. Of course, private ownership is tolerated to a degree, but that degree is strictly limited by the elimination of rent and wages. Even self-employment is restricted, for the *Green Book* disallows savings from surplus over needs (however they may be defined).

Land, the *Green Book* says, belongs to everyone. Advocates of Islamic socialism generally say it belongs to God; other Muslims believe the Quran protects the right of private ownership. The *Green Book* says anyone may claim land in order to work it — as long as this does not involve exploitation (rent or wages), a stricture which goes far beyond all other Arab socialisms. By comparison, Nasser's land reform program, after promulgation of three laws which successively reduced the limits on private ownership, still permitted fifty acres for a personal holding, although 95% of landowners owned less than five acres.

Islam accepts the naturalness of rich and poor in society, and requires that the rich become the benefactors of society, that is, that they accept responsibility commensurate with their wealth, a notion familiar to European aristocracy under the heading of *noblesse oblige*. And of course, responsibility is a basis of power. The poor have the right to be the beneficiaries of society, so the transfer of alms deserves no gratitude. El-Qaddafi goes far beyond the Quran: charity, like wages, can be withheld or withdrawn; both are insidious and must be abolished. But the *Green Book,* in a sense, reflects the Quran in rewarding the benefactors of society with extra wealth, about the only mention of a possibility of unequal income not based on unequal need. The *Green Book's* reference to charity is certainly meant as a reference to charity in capitalist society which demeans the recipient as it glorifies the donor, whereas the Islamic obligation of almsgiving is a duty to God.

While the question is clearly not to be answered decisively from perusal of the *Green Book,* it appears that after allowing for the many parallels between el-Qaddafi's "Third Universal Theory" and the teachings of Islam, it cannot be stated that the Third Universal Theory derives exclusively from Islam; unlike nearly all the other works extolling an Islamic socialism by progressive Islamicists, the *Green Book* recognizes no need to distinguish clearly doctrinal differences between Jamahiriya socialism and Marxism. One has the impression that for el-Qaddafi there are no real conflicts. The Libyan case is unique; Libya is basically still a tribal society, tentatively mobilized into a nation under the charismatic leadership of Sufi masters to resist foreign domination and colonial pressures. Its bourgeoisie is largely foreign, its economy and commerce controlled until the 1970s by foreign oil companies. Libya's 1969 coup under Colonel el-Qaddafi and the other young officers was largely inspired by Nasser's coup in Egypt in 1952. More a visionary than Nasser was, el-Qaddafi and his democratic socialist experiment appear as radical as Muhammad's idea of an Islamic state must have. It is clear that Muhammad's following was due to his political genius.

El-Qaddafi in many ways resembles the Prophet, and his task is not altogether unlike the earlier one of Muhammad: to draw upon the accumulated wisdom of civilizations that had once had vigor, and by providing these with a wholly new social organization, to produce, phoenix-like, a new potential for humans to achieve that which their Creator had intended for them. But in other ways, one is impressed with the similarities of el-Qaddafi's and Mao's effects on the masses. China's Great Leap Forward began with great bursts of enthusiasm and may have burned itself out from the sheer energy expended in slogans, marching songs, and mass motion. It is not unthinkable that the situation today in Libya is a polarization of the "Green" versus "experts" factions — except that in Libya's case, experts are still foreigners, easily sent away whenever the country can do without them. The real question is: is the Guru of Libya the only true socialist in the country? Is he naive or very wise in thinking he can combine Arabism, socialism, and a radical form of democracy with Islamic morality, without mentioning any of these by name — in other words, by issuing what may be taken to be a direct message, through this religious mystic, from God? Few take Muaamar el-Qaddafi and his Third Universal Theory seriously. Syria is seriously considering a merger as this is being written, yet that sort of thing has happened many times with the same dismal results. There is something enigmatic about one who can combine a Marxist-style view of history with a fundamentalist's morality. Is the term "universal" a reference to God's message, timeless and everywhere applicable? Or is the reference to the inevitable replacement of human solutions by others, the "dialectic" process which will replace capitalism and communism by a new society of vaguely understood characteristics?

Islam and Modern Education

If el-Qaddafi's program is too radical to be truly an Islamic solution, are there other contenders? It appears that while there are advocates in many places, the design of such an Islamic solution is still on the drawing boards. We mean by drawing boards the Muslim universities and the attempts by scholars who treat seriously the possibility of an Islamic society to endow the Islamic movement with modern intellectual tools. These are tools which the theologian cannot provide, only the specialist trained in modern (Western) theory and method.

An example is the development for Aligarh Muslim University (India) of a curriculum at the graduate level in Islamic economics. What would such a curriculum teach? First, it would have to develop a critical awareness, says one Muslim scholar, that modern economics, as taught in the West and imported to the Muslim world, is essentially capitalist economics, developed in the historical context of developing capitalist society, and "fitting" those societies (Britain and, later, the U.S.) but not necessarily all societies. When one analyzes the concepts of neoclassical or marginalist economics critically, these concepts seem less logically necessary than sociologically required: they serve to legitimize cultural emphases of these societies and undermine opposite emphases by the very form of their analysis. For example, individualism is built into microanalysis, distribution is virtually ignored, as is the role of the state in economic management — except perhaps for the odd course in welfare economics.

If capitalist economics will not serve well the development needs of Third World countries, especially Muslim countries, then a new economics must be developed. Professor Siddiqi of Aligarh Muslim University has outlined such a curriculum.[43] To develop an economic theory that is free of "capitalist" bias, he suggest scrutinizing the core concepts of modern economic theory in the light of Islamic values. He notes in passing that substituting Marxist economics for "capitalist" economics is no solution, but merely ends in a second kind of excess: making the individual, not the motive force in the economy, but "a passive agent not to be trusted with freedom" which does not "suit the temper of the Islamic peoples."[44]

An example of Dr. Siddiqi's revisionism is with respect to the concept of "capital" as a separate factor of production. He notes that Islam does not recognize capital's claim to a guaranteed positive return in the form of interest,[45] and finds it essential to distinguish between risk capital, which deserves the interest paid on it, and loan capital, which does not, since payment is guaranteed. Modern theory treats interest as an item of cost and ascribes it to the productivity of capital, not because this makes analytical sense but because capitalist society approves the institution of interest, and then requires the productivity of capital in order to legitimize this interest payment, reversing the actual relationship.

Sounding very much like Marxist critics, Dr. Siddiqi suggests the need for a critical review of numerous concepts, including development, money, income, employment, and a host of others.

Like Marxist economics, Islamic economics may have a greater impact as normative sociology than as an analytical apparatus, for Dr. Siddiqi's suggestions include taking into account "noneconomic" social institutions and values as well as nonworldly goals. Some areas of the total curriculum would remain unchanged, e.g., quantitative methods. The changes from the Western-derived curriculum would be reflected in courses on micro- and macrotheory, the history of Islamic economic thought, and economic history. The last would be taught to incorporate revisions that reflect both the revised concepts (such as "capital") and the revised interpretations of history from a Muslim Third World viewpoint. Such a curriculum would treat special problems of Islamic countries, not in terms of a theory adapted to justifying Western colonialism, but in terms of a theory consistent with the goals of an Islamic society. Examples of such problems could include the role of money and banking in a *zakat*-based economy, the role of government in Muslim countries with expanding public sectors, and so on.

It is clear that the education of the "new Muslim," according to scholars such as Dr. Siddiqi, is part of a moral reform which contrasts with the revolutionary changes already underway in Libya. What may deserve our attention is the fact that Muslim scholars, taking the idea of an Islamic society and an Islamic state seriously, are moving to equip such an eventuality with a kit of modern intellectual tools. They are finding theoretical support from Dependency Theory writings of Westerners who warn that Western "bourgeois" theory interprets the oppression of people as the fault of the victims; but they have rejected the solutions of the Marxists as equally alien and unfit. Thus, where Western-bloc and Eastern-bloc economists may agree on a classification of world economies as capitalist, socialist, and "mixed" (implying that all viable alternatives have been tried), these Muslim economists aim at a third type, the Islamic Economy, worthy of its own label because it is something new, as well as something traditional.

The development of an Islamic economics may be seen as a second step, with recent revisionist histories regarded as the first step to a modern Islamic curriculum. But what about the possibility of a modern Islamic philosophy? Beneath all of the legal diversity of interpretation, the accommodation to local traditions, the sectarian differences arising out of political conflict, the Sufi movements against a growing formalism and dying spirituality, the movements to reform, to "intellectualize," and to "purify" Islam, is there a common philosophical view on, say, human nature, the nature of human relations, the relations between man and environment which could provide a cosmology, an ethic, a metaphysic consistent with the development needs of Muslim countries? Western social philosophies have been polarized as "individualist" and "collectivist." Where does Islam stand on these in general? Islamic philosophers reject the claims of the two Western social philosophies regarding individual rights and collective welfare respectively. They insist that Islam offers a happy medium between these extremes, yet not a compromise between the two "Western" traditions, which remain in the end more similar to each other than either resembles the Islamic world view. Both are basically materialist philosophies and are monist in their views of reality. Western idealism is not a solution, for it rejects the importance of economic relations and is just as firmly monist as is materialism; the only difference lies in fact that to the materialist, ideas are mere reflections of the material reality, while to the idealist, the reality is a mere projection of the ideational reality.[47] Islam, in contrast, opposes materialism because it rejects monism in favor of an explicit dualism. For Islam, the reality of God and matter are equal. God created heaven and earth with *haq* (reality) inherent in them.

Modernist Islam, then, has no quarrel with scientific theories such as Darwinian evolution, nor even with cultural/social evolution based on material causation — up to a point. But that point is critical: it is the point at which divine intervention inspires Man to become a special creation, still an animal responding to its environment, yes, but not *only* an animal — a special creature capable of inspired acts which permit it to go beyond mere environmental limits. In other words, Islam preserves the "great man" theories of historical change, regarding them not as opposed to deterministic theories of material casuality but simply as a supplement: the addition of divine inspiration through faith. Islam and liberal Christian thought merge on this issue.

Thus, in spite of situational limitations, certain human consciousnesses have *transcended* mundane limits, not disproving natural laws but rather proving the existence of divine inspiration, the existence of God. Abraham, Moses, Jesus, Muhammad were all examples of divinely inspired creativity. But Muhammad was the last Prophet, so large doses of inspiration cannot be counted on in future. Instead, the concerted, thoughtful, somewhat inspired cooperative endeavor of humans will be required.

For this, a modernized Islamic rationality is felt by its advocates to be superior in strength to that of Western *Homo oeconomicus*. It will have to be a rationality modernized not in the manner of al-Afghani and M. Abduh, not by applying measures which derive from Western rationalism, but rather one that is historically derived from Muslims' experience, that can be interpreted critically and still applied positively to constructing the future. It is not that skeptics find it inconceivable that religion can *serve* ends which are progressive; the challenge of progressive Islam is that it offers to *explain* these ends. History will be the judge of its success.

Islam: The Legal Dimension

by Safia K. Mohsen

A sense of excitement hung over the public square as young men and boys ran about trying to find out what was happening. A caravan of luxurious cars arrived, stirring the dust on the unpaved roads leading to the square. A figure draped in black was dragged out of one of the cars by two men. The figure staggered as it was led to one side of the square and propped against a small mound of sand. The sound of gunfire was heard and the dark figure collapsed to the ground. This was the *Death of a Princess.* This scene from the controversial film shown on many television stations in the United States and some European countries, and the reports of trials and executions by Iranian Islamic courts for both political and non-political crimes, have tended to reinforce a Western image of Islamic justice as a medieval system that holds no respect for individual rights and freedoms.

This view is by no means restricted to the West. Many non-Western societies and groups within the Islamic societies themselves have long held the view that certain aspects of Islamic law are incompatible with modern living, that it was created to suit the social and political needs of Arabia at the time of the Prophet and does not meet the demands and requirements of the complex social systems of the twentieth century. The prevalence of such views has resulted in the abandoning of some or all aspects of Islamic law by many Muslim countries.

Until about a century ago Islamic law was the main source of legislation in the Middle East. As Muslim societies in that area began to revise their legal codes, they shifted away from Islamic sources and toward Western legal systems, mainly the Napoleonic Code. Among the first to be abandoned were administrative, constitutional, and criminal laws which, it was argued, required rules of procedures and/or evidence that were too cumbersome for the complex life of modern societies. This was also true with commercial law; the Islamic prohibition of usury and of speculative contracts was viewed as too restricting to the types of transactions characteristic of contemporary economic life in the Middle East. The *Sharia*

99

remained, however, in the background as the ultimate guide of social interaction.

The basic legacy of Islamic law was in the form of secular courts and secular laws to function side by side with the Sharia courts. The Ottomans enacted a commercial code in 1850, derived for the most part from the Napoleonic Code. Secular courts, mixed courts for cases involving foreigners, and *nizami* courts for cases involving only Ottoman subjects, were established to deal with the new laws.

The only aspects of Islamic law that still apply in the majority of the countries in the Middle East are those pertaining to personal status and family affairs. Even these have undergone drastic modifications in countries such as Tunisia, where their connection to Islamic law has become merely symbolic.

On the other hand, a few countries have retained Islamic law as the major source of their legislation. Notable among them is Saudi Arabia. The Saudi system of criminal justice has recently provided inspiration for those groups within other societies in the area who call for a reinstatement of Islamic law. Motivated by ideological bias against the West and its institutions, including the legal institutions, or by simple anxiety over the increase in crime and violence in their societies, groups within countries such as Iran, Libya, and Egypt have called for major legislative changes to reflect more of the Islamic nature of these societies. Some of these efforts have been successful, as in the case of Iran; in Egypt, a recent referendum showed that the vast majority of those who voted favored a major legislative revision to reinstate Islamic law as *the* major source of legislation. This has revived the debate over the place of Islamic law in contemporary Islamic societies. The aim of this paper is to provide an understanding of the nature of this debate by examining certain aspects of Islamic law, especially in the two controversial areas of criminal justice, and of personal status and family regulations.

The Historic Context of Islamic Legislation

Individualism did not exist in pre-Islamic Arabia. Legally, politically and socially, the individual was inseparable from the group to which he belonged. The agnatic group bore responsibility for crimes committed by the individual, especially those involving liabilities for death or personal injury, and it was the agency for retribution for death or injury suffered by its members. A criminal law in the sense of a public law with the state as the prime legal agency was unknown. There were only private wrongs and private methods to deal with them. In such a system, the individual was legally indistinguishable from the kin group. A person who did not belong to a group was without any legal protection, and one of the most severe penalties a group could impose upon its members was that of ostracism; it meant that acts of violence against him were not avenged.

The importance of the kinship group was also evident in the political sphere. There was no political authority above the kinship groupings. Those autonomous units, varying in size and power, provided the political framework of Arabian society. Several treaties and federations did exist between some of these tribes or clans, but they were more on the order of foreign treaties of modern time than a permanent internal political organization of that period.

Such political fragmentation was reflected in religious diversity. Each of the major tribes worshiped its own idols, which were kept, however, in Mecca, a thriving commercial center at the time. Protection for the idols was provided by the powerful Meccan tribe of Quraysh (to which the Prophet Muhammad belonged). A free zone (*haram* area) in which fighting was prohibited surrounded the place where the idols were kept and permitted free visitation of members of all tribes to the shrine. Protection was also provided for individuals with no tribal affiliation. Those were either members of local groups who were ousted by their own tribe, or foreigners who had no tribal affiliation in the area. Thus a form of citizenship existed in Mecca at the time of Muhammad. While citizens of Mecca enjoyed freedom from domination by their groups, Meccan political structure was far from equitable. In contrast to the egalitarianism of the tribal organization, Meccan society was highly stratified.

> While the rich merchants were increasing their personal wealth, they were also more and more disregarding their obligations toward the less fortunate members of their clan or family. The capital which had formed the basis of their earliest trading operations was probably the communal wealth of the group, of which they were only administrators; but the profits went into their own pockets, and before long there was no communal property left. Those in a socially weak position, notably widows and orphans, were shamelessly cheated and oppressed. . . .[1]

Thus in Mecca individualism gained at the expense of egalitarianism. In his formulation of the Islamic community, Muhammad had two models: that of the politically and religiously fragmented, but egalitarian, kinship-based society of the tribal groups outside Mecca; and the individualistic, politically integrated, but highly stratified Meccan society. The aim of Muhammad was to create a new order which took the best of both systems, while avoiding the liabilities of either. Such a society was to provide a wider political integration and liberate the individual from the domination of the kinship groups, while maintaining an egalitarian ideology and a sense of social responsibility.

This seemingly impossible task was achieved through the concept of the *umma,* or Islamic community. The umma is a political entity made up of individuals and held together by common allegiance to God, and to his ideals revealed to his messenger Muhamed. The umma is not a territorial unit but a community of believers. By relating the individual directly to God without the mediation of any group, Islam aimed at reducing the hold the group had over the individual, incorporating him/her as an individual in a wider and more effective political structure. The underlying assumption of that individualistic trend is that all individuals are equal in the eyes of God: "All of you are like the teeth of a comb, no one is distinguished from the other except by the strength of his belief."

> In its internal aspect, the Umma consisted of the totality of individuals bound to one another by ties not of kinship or race, but of religion, in that all its members profess their belief in one God, Allah, and in the mission of his prophet, Muhammad. . . . Before God and in relation to him, all are equal without distinction of rank, class or race. . . .[2]

The mechanism whereby the umma was to be achieved was an elaborate "legal" system known as the Sharia (the legitimate path) which organized and regulated the behavior of individuals, in both their relationship to one another, and their relationship to God. The lack of separation in the umma between the political, social, and religious spheres has extended the Sharia rules over a much wider area of human activities than those generally covered by "modern" (secular) legal systems. To many Western readers, Islamic law seems too preoccupied with the details of day-to-day activities.

The method of establishing the new Islamic community was unique for a revolutionary movement. Although the aim was to create a new and different social and moral order, the destruction of the old one was not a prerequisite for such a process. Instead, emphasis was on retaining those aspects of the old structure that were either compatible with, or could be modified to fit, the basic ideals of the new society. For those aspects that were considered in direct conflict with the new system, the process of prohibiting them was a slow and gradual one (this was the case with drinking alcohol, which passed through four phases from complete license to total prohibition). The justification was that drastic and rapid changes in the way people live would create unnecessary hardship and were likely to create resistance to the new ideas. Muhammad, then, recognized the importance of tradition in the shaping of social reality, and he used that understanding in his efforts to shape the Islamic community.

As a result of that strategy, many of the old practices and concepts found their way into Islamic law, and it is the persistence of some of these practices that provides the basis for criticism by those who maintain that Islamic law is incompatible with the needs of modern times.

Crime and Punishment in Islam: Criminal Law

Islam identified certain activities as being incompatible with the ideal of the Islamic community. To discourage individuals from pursuing such activities, Islam succeeded in the following:

1) It developed internal control to prevent people from committing crimes. Such control was achieved through religious teaching aimed at establishing a just society and at creating social interdependence that develops a sense of communal responsibility. The idea was to establish a type of society in which no one could prosper at the expense of others (*riba*), in which no one should go hungry while others have more than they need (*zakah*), in which charity and peace are the underlying foundations of human interaction, and in which everyone is equal in the eyes of God. It is important to note here that by "equality" Islam did not mean an equal distribution of wealth and/or power but a system of allocation of social responsibilities proportionate to one's prominence in society. Thus the wealthier and more powerful individuals are expected to contribute to their communities both wealth and social involvement, and to provide models to be followed by the poor and the less affluent. For this reason, they become subject to harsher legal penalties for their

crimes. Such harsh treatment—especially when the penalties are financial—is also based on the principle of equal "burden" or "hardship" of the criminal penalties in Islamic law.

2) It created a public opinion which discourages the violation of the Sharia rules. This is achieved through a general command to the Muslims to advise those whose behavior violates the ideals of the Muslim community or which represents danger to its image. This general obligation aims at establishing public pressure against those who are inclined to violate the law. Thus, Islam gives an important role to group pressure as a means to establish compliance with its basic tenets, and makes it an effective way to control deviation.

3) It established effective punishment of the violators. In addition to the vaguely defined religious sanctions anticipated in any case of violation of Islamic teachings, certain areas of human activities were considered vital enough to the existence of Islamic community that they were also protected by secular (worldly) sanctions. These are for the most part acts considered detrimental to the public interest, or acts involving serious infringement upon the rights of the individuals. This is the domain of Islamic criminal law.

Four areas are identified by Islamic law as prime targets for legal protection:

1) The first and most vital is *religion*. While the aim is to provide the believers with the proper atmosphere for practicing Islam, it recognizes and protects the right of individuals to follow religions other than Islam. Freedom of religion under Islam has strong support in several statements in the *Quran* and *Sunna* which instruct the believers that there should be "no coercion in Islam." This protection however, does not extend to those who abandon Islam, for *ridda,* or apostasy, is one of the most serious crimes in Islamic law.

2) *Individual safety.* This includes protection of the person's body as well as his/her dignity. This latter is defined in terms of the right to be protected against public insults and humiliation, the right to work, the right to express one's thoughts without fear of reprisal, the right to chose one's residence, and "all other rights and freedoms considered essential for living free in a moral society. . . . and as long as the exercise of these rights does not infringe upon the rights of others in their exercise of their rights."[3] Such rights, however, do not apply equally to all members of the society. For example, women's right to work as well as their freedom of movement

are limited by the right of their husbands to prevent them from leaving the house without permission, except in cases specified by law, a point which will be covered later in the chapter.

Protection of the individual's safety and security extends to his/her mental and psychological health. Thus the use of substances that are known to affect the human mind and to interfere with one's ability to exercise sound judgments are also prohibited.

3) *Descent and procreation.* The protection of this vital area of human activities is maintained through the detailed regulation of marriage and family affairs, and through the criminalization of sexual unions outside the domain of marriage.

4) *Property and wealth.* The protection of private property is one of the main foci of Islamic law. Acts that deprive the individual of his/her rightfully owned property are subject to severe punishment.

Acts that threaten these areas are deemed "criminal" by Islamic law. Such criminal acts are in turn classified into two categories: crimes against the rights of God (*hudud*; in the singular: *hadd*) and crimes against the rights of human beings (*ta'zir*). The first category covers areas considered essential for the maintenance of public morality and the protection of basic Islamic values. Some of the prohibited acts do not involve the victimization of any individuals, as in the case of sexual relations between unmarried consenting adults. However, they are considered enough of a threat to the Muslim family to be criminalized.

But even when crimes in this category are committed against individuals—theft, for example—the rights of the victims are subsumed by those of God. Since God is the symbol of the Islamic community, such crimes come very close to the modern legal system's conception of crimes as "public wrongs."

The term "hudud" refers to both the crimes themselves as well as to the type of punishment designated for them. These punishments are rigidly and specifically defined and, therefore, leave little room for the discretionary powers of the judges. The judge's role in this area is largely limited to the assessment of guilt or innocence. Once guilt is established, the judge has no alternative but to impose the penalty as defined. Of course, in assessing the guilt, the judge may take into consideration any conditions relating to either the crime or the offender. Thus a confessed thief may be judged innocent if the judge is convinced that he was compelled to steal to feed himself or his family. Because of the importance of the areas covered by the hudud, and the nature of the penalties designed for them, they are strictly defined and rules of evidence and procedures required for conviction are spelled out in detail. Six crimes are defined as hudud in Islam:

Apostasy: The death penalty for the man who abandons Islam is one of the harshest penalties in Islamic law. To explain the apparent contradiction between "the religion of tolerance," as Islam is commonly called, and the harsh penalty assigned for conversion from Islam, some jurists maintain that the legal prohibition is designed not to curb the religious freedom of the individual but to discourage false conversion to Islam in the first place. They argue that some might take advantage of the relative informality and ease of conversion to Islam to gain temporary personal advantage without really being a true believer in the new religion. Some whose religion does not permit polygyny or divorce may convert to Islam just to take advantage of Islamic rules of marriage and divorce. Harsh penalties for apostasy discourage such false conversion and protect the integrity of the religion.

Adultery: Islamic law considers as adultery any sexual act between a man and a woman unsanctioned by marriage. This includes relationships involving married as well as unmarried individuals. Despite the fact that such acts may not involve the victimization of a person, as in the case of sexual relationships between unmarried consenting adults, Islam considers adultery a major threat to the one institution most vital to the survival of the Islamic community, the family.

> . . . If these relationships (adulterous) were to prevail people will abandon marriage . . . the family will disintegrate and along with it the strongest bond in any decent society. . . . A nation in which adultery is widespread is destined for destruction, decrease in population, and enmity among its men . . . adultery is similar to murder except that it is directed not only against one life but against many lives. . . .[4]

For this reason, Islamic law reserves one of its harshest penalties for adultery, especially for those involving married individuals. The penalty is stoning for married individuals and eighty lashes for unmarried individuals. Despite recent publicity given to some cases of stoning in Iran, actual cases of stoning have been rare in the history of Islamic legal procedures. As with the cases of all hudud crimes, strict rules of evidence are required. To discourage false accusation of women of adultery, Islamic law requires that four credible witnesses swear to having observed the sexual act. No circumstantial evidence, no matter how strong, could be accepted for such accusation. Failure to produce such evidence may subject the informers to the harsh penalty of the crime of slander (another hadd). A husband can, however, accuse his wife of adultery, without providing the necessary witnesses, by swearing four times that she committed the act. In this case, a wife can exonerate herself by swearing "four times plus one" that she was innocent of the accusation.

In practice, conviction for adultery has been restricted, for the most part, to cases where the individuals involved confessed voluntarily to their commission of the act. Such cases are rare, if we consider that Islam does not encourage confession of crimes. This will be discussed later.

Intoxication: Islamic law does not draw a distinction between alcohol and mind-altering drugs. Both substances are prohibited. The original prohibition, however, was restricted to alcohol. The use of drugs was not prevalent during the early phases of Islam, when the legal provisions were established. When later the use of drugs became more common, and their effects on the human mind were recognized, the rules applying to alcohol were extended to include drugs as well.

The prohibition of alcohol was established gradually in Islamic law. At the beginning of Islam, the use of alcohol was so widespread and accepted that it was feared that prohibition would create resistance to, and resentment of, the new religion, and alcohol was, therefore, permitted. Thus the Quran states "And from the fruit of the palm tree and the vine you were given intoxicants (*sakar*) and good food. . . ."[5] The first prohibition came in the form of a warning to the believers that although alcohol was permitted, it had evil and harmful effects. "They ask you about intoxicants (*khamr*) and games of chance . . . say they are harmful as well as beneficial . . . but their harm exceeds their benefits."[6]

The next phase was one in which alcohol, still allowed, was not permitted before prayers.

"O believers, do not pray while intoxicated so you can realize what you are saying. . . ."[7]

A man was considered intoxicated if he "became incoherent, could not distinguish a man from a woman, the sky from the earth or himself from a donkey."[8] Total prohibition of alcohol came about presumably because the above warnings did not produce the desired results. A clear prohibition was communicated to Muhammad in Sura *al-Maida* which states "O believers, intoxicants and gambling . . . are the work of the devil, so avoid them . . ."[9]

While Islamic jurists are in general agreement that alcohol is prohibited, they disagree on several points regarding the nature of this prohibition. One of these points is the definition of alcohol. Another is the question of what is criminalized. Except for the Hanafi school of jurisprudence, there is a general agreement among jurists that alcohol is any drink that affects the mental capacity of the individual. The Hanafis, on the other hand, consider as alcohol only those drinks made from grapes. Such drinks, even when taken in moderation, are forbidden. On the other hand, the Hanafis maintain that other drinks are permitted until they cause intoxication. In the latter case, then, the prohibition applies only to the state of intoxication and not to the mere act of drinking. One reference supporting these views indicated that Ali used to offer wine to his guests, then prosecute those who became drunk. When the guests protested on the basis that it was he, the leader of the Islamic community, that offered the drinks, his answer was, "the punishment is not for drinking, it is for being drunk."[10] It is this view that is expressed by those Muslims in contemporary Middle Eastern societies who do drink alcohol. "As long as I am not making a fool of myself," said one of them, "I am not violating Islamic proscriptions. Besides, I am drinking for health reasons. I digest my food better."

Most jurists follow the Prophet's dictum that any drinks which cause intoxication when drunk in large quantities, are also prohibited in small quantities. Some maintain that only "strong" drinks are prohibited, while other insist that since Muhammad mentioned only drinks from grapes and palm trees, other drinks, no matter how strong, should not be subject to the prohibition.[11] This, again, is taken by some contemporary Muslims to indicate that beer, a popular drink in the Middle East, is not included in the Islamic prohibition.

Whatever the legal injunctions, the social reality indicates that this is one Islamic prohibition that is not uniformly followed in the Muslim world. Nor is that a recent phenomenon. Arabic literature is abundant with references to drinking. In fact a type of poetry (*al-khamriyyat*, wine poetry) is devoted to the state of drinking.

History books are full of references to Muslims, especially those in leadership positions, who drank and served drinks to their guests. There are indications of the widespread use of alcohol from the beginning of the Ummayyad rule.

Despite the lack of a specific reference in the Quran prohibiting the use of drugs, such use was also prohibited in later periods through the application of the rule of analogy which extended the prohibition of alcohol to the use of drugs. The justification is that drugs have the same effect on the human mind as alcohol, and they therefore produce the same public harm that led to the prohibition of the former.

As with alcohol, drug prohibition is the subject of debate among jurists who disagree on what should be included as drugs to be prohibited. Despite its illegality in all Muslim countries, the use of such a substance as hashish or opium is not viewed by the public as the same as alcohol. Many devout Muslims who would not consider drinking alcohol would not see anything wrong in the use of hashish or opium.

For both alcohol and drugs, Islam does not punish those who are addicted to them. While addicts are denied a place in heaven because they are the same as "idol worshipers," Islam does recognize that they are compelled to use the substance. In such cases it allows the usage by the addict on the condition that the user gradually reduce the amount until he is cured of the dependency. When he reaches that state, it becomes prohibited for him. The law, then, treats the addict's use of drugs or alcohol as medical treatment similar to the use of drugs to cure other ailments.

Slander: This hadd is restricted to false accusation of adultery. The victim may be a man or a woman. While this crime seems directly aimed at the rights of the individual, it is also considered as a violation of the right of God because of its implication for public morality and the basic ideals of the Islamic community. According to Islamic jurists, if such a crime is not effectively discouraged, rumors will go unchecked and will be treated as fact, thereby creating an impression of an immoral society. Moreover, it tends to undermine the authority of the leaders or those in a position of power. Anyone who accuses another of adultery without providing conclusive evidence is subject to the hadd, which is eighty lashes. In addition, the slanderer losses his right to testify in any legal case.

Theft: To the Western reader, the cutting off of the hand of the thief symbolizes Islamic criminal justice, an evidence of its lack of compassion and its disregard for the sanctity of the human body, for no matter how great the monetary loss is, it cannot be compared with the permanent loss of a limb. This especially confuses those who are familiar with the Islamic principle of criminal justice which states that the punishment should be proportionate to the harm done by the crime. It will also seem puzzling to many why a crime that is directed almost exclusively against the individual's right to private property should be considered as a crime against the rights of God. One may be tempted to interpret it as an indication of the importance Islam gives to the protection of property rights, except that other acts that violate these rights, such as fraud and embezzlement, are not as harshly treated in Islamic law.

Islamic jurists maintain that the reason for including theft in the hudud is based not on the monetary loss involved, but on the public fear and disorder the crime generates.

> . . . prevalence of theft has far reaching social implications . . . one case of theft in a village or a neighborhood disturbs the peace and quiet of the area. People will resort to guards, doors, locks and a state of fear would prevail. . . . [besides] thieves always prey upon the weak, women and the defenseless, usually at night invading their sleeping quarters, depriving them of their money and jewelry and frequently killing them in the process. . . ."[12]

Because of the severity of the punishment for theft, however, Islamic law narrowly defines theft (acts subject to the application of the hadd) by setting strict limits for defining possession and ownership. Therefore the law requires that for an item to be considered stolen, the thief must remove it from the locality in which the theft has allegedly taken place. Ownership of the stolen property is also strictly defined for the purpose of the application of the theft hadd. Some jurists maintain that things that were originally part of nature, such as game animals and fish, cannot be "stolen," even after they become the private property of the person who hunted or fished them. The same applies to pearls and rare stones of various kinds. Stealing from the public treasury is not subject to the hadd (although it may be punishable by another provision in Islamic law), on the assumption that it belongs to all members of the community including the thief. Some jurists also maintain that no hadd can be applied in the case of stealing perishables such as meat, eggs, or other food items, while others insist that any item that is of public use, even if privately owned, cannot be stolen. This applies to the theft of religious items such as copies of the Quran. Still others require a minimum value for the item stolen to be subject to the hadd prohibition. Finally, the hadd for theft, as for all other crimes in Islamic law, cannot be applied if the crime was committed under compelling reasons. In the case of theft, a person should not be punished if he/she stole food to feed himself or his family. In the latter case, however, the items stolen should be just enough to ward off the hunger.

Banditry: The same reasons for including theft in the hudud crimes apply to the crime of banditry. But in addition, banditry represents a direct challenge to the authority of the state. For this reason it carries a much harsher penalty than the one designated for theft.

> Those who challenge the authority of God and his prophet and spread corruption on earth shall be crucified, have their alternate arms and legs cut off, or exiled. Such is their humiliation in life, and great suffering awaits them on the day of judgement. . . .[13]

Deterrence, then, is the underlying principle of the punishment in the case of the hudud and is given precedent over the principle of *balance,* which is the basis of punishment in crimes against the rights of individuals. These acts have been exempt from the more basic principle of *balance* between the crime and punishment by the fact that they represent a direct threat to the authority and legitimacy of the state and to the leaders. While the hudud cannot be expanded by definition, the philosophy of deterrence in the cases of crimes that threaten the authority of the Islamic leadership can be seen in the harsh punishments imposed in recent months by the Iranian revolutionary courts for relatively minor offenses such as prostitution and drugs. Crimes that symbolize Western decadence have become a direct threat to the purity of the Islamic revolution, and that revolution claims legitimacy by rejecting Western "morality." The reference to "corruption on earth" in the Quranic statement regarding banditry could be widely interpreted to include any crime that threatens the authority of the government or weakens the moral foundation of the Islamic community.

Deterrence can be achieved by a few publicized cases. Therefore, Islamic jurists maintain that the hudud punishments should be applied very infrequently: ". . . the important thing is publicity associated with the application of the punishment, regardless of how many hands are cut off."[14]

The importance of deterrence in the above crimes has led the Islamic legislature in these cases to discourage compassion and forgiveness, two of the most important precepts in Islamic teaching. Realizing that the discrepancy between what the public may perceive as the immediate harm caused by the crime, and the penalty imposed, might lead the public to call for leniency in these crimes, Islam warns against such an attitude in applying the hudud.

"... the adulteress and her partner, each should receive one hundred lashes. Do not have pity or compassion for them if you believe in God and the day of judgement. . . ."[15]

Except for the six crimes mentioned above, all crimes are considered violations of the rights of individuals. This is not to imply that they do not jeopardize the interest of the group, for all crimes threaten the public order if left unchecked. What is meant is that, unlike hudud, where the rights of God are given precedence over the rights of individuals, the ta'zir crimes leave some leeway to the aggrieved parties, as well as to the judges, to negotiate a satisfactory sentence. The aim of the penalty in these crimes is to calm the feelings of the victim and/or his relatives. For this reason the emphasis is on *balance* between the harm done and the penalty imposed. Therefore, an eye for an eye and a tooth for a tooth is the basic principle. Leniency and forgiveness, discouraged in the hudud, are encouraged in the crimes against individuals.

The fact that crimes in Islamic law include both public as well as private wrongs distinguishes Islamic law from modern secular criminal laws, as in Egypt and elsewhere. The latter are public laws. This means that crimes by definition are offenses against society, not merely violations of the private rights of an individual or group of individuals. Therefore, in exacting the punishment, the victim and/or his kinship group have no role in either the determination of the punishment or in carrying it out. Thus no victim of assault or the relatives of a murder victim can "pardon" the murderer or stop the legal proceedings against him. A few minor exceptions do exist in some modern legal systems. In the Egyptian criminal code (derived mainly from the Napoleonic Code) the husband of a convicted adulteress can stop the sentence against her at any time by simply agreeing to resume the marital relationship with her. Such cases, however, are rare and are almost always relatively minor offenses involving relationships within the domestic domain.

In the process of consolidating the power of the state, modern criminal laws have tended to go to the extreme of reifying "society" to the neglect of the rights and the feelings of the victim as an individual. On the other hand, social and political awareness has tended to emphasize the contribution of society to the deviation of the criminal, and tended to see him as, in some way, a victim himself. The degree of democracy has recently been measured by the legal guarantees of the rights and freedom of the accused. In the zeal of certain legal institutions to provide safeguards for the accused, the interests or the feelings of the victim and/or his family have been forgotten. The rights of the accused have become individualized, while the rights of the victim have become collectivized and incorporated into the rights of society. In the United States, the neglect of the victim's rights and feelings have been stressed in a chart, put together by the Law Enforcement Assistance Administration (LEAA), titled "The Criminal Injustice System." It states that, if arrested, the criminal will be informed of his/her rights, and if injured will get medical attention at the expense of the state, that he will be provided with an attorney if he cannot afford one, and that he may be released on bail. The victim, on the other hand, pays his own medical bills, and is often required to give up time and energy to aid in the investigation, which frequently ends with very light sentences. As the director of the victim-witness program in Alameda County, California put it, "The system as it is does not treat victims like people, it treats them as though they were burglar tools or a stolen television set, just another piece of evidence."[16]

Islamic criminal law takes an opposite position with regard to the attitude toward both the victim and the offender. Having established a just society, Islam absolves the collectivity from any responsibility for the acts of the criminal. His crime is considered a product of his own evil and corrupt mind and not of the social conditions surrounding him. The criminal becomes a direct threat to the moral order of the society, and the aim of the law is to prevent him from continuing his activities on the one hand, and to deter others from following suit on the other.

The Islamic idea of punishment is mostly that of deterrence. But the crime, while representing a threat to the public order, is also directed against specific individuals. Their feelings and their need for revenge should also be considered. This is particularly important in the case of crimes that cause physical harm to the victims, such as murder and assault. In these cases, Islamic law gives the victim and/or his relatives a decisive role in determining the penalty and in carrying it out. This does not mean that the state leaves the entire process of criminal justice in these cases in the hands of the aggrieved parties or their relatives. Unlike the pre-Islamic system of vengeance, which operated in total absence of a state legal structure, Islam has divided the responsibility for vegeance between the state and the aggrieved parties. The state evaluates the evidence and establishes the guilt or innocence of the accused. It also defines the type of punishment to be applied. But the carrying out of the sentence is left to the discretion of the victim and/or his relatives. Thus in the case of murder, the victim's kin group must abide by the decision of the legal authority as to whether the penalty should be the payment of blood money. But it is up to the latter to decide whether they carry out the sentence or commute it. While they can commute a sentence, the group cannot exceed the penalty specified by the court. A death sentence may be substituted by the payment of blood money, or dropped altogether, but a sentence of blood money may not be turned into a death sentence by the victim's group.

It has almost always been the case that the victim or his group received compensation for the harm done to them by the offender. For this reason Islam did not look with favor on imprisonment as a viable penalty. It was considered incompatible with the philosophy of punishment in Islam. It is demeaning to the offender to be caged like an animal, it is costly to maintain, and it does not help to calm the feelings of the victim. Moreover, it does not provide the deterrent element so essential to the concept of legal punishment in Islam. Since it is not public and extends over a period of time, it is difficult to associate the hardship of the penalty with the crime committed.

The emphasis Islamic law puts upon individual rights has led to another characteristic of Islamic criminal justice that distinguishes it from modern legal systems. The individual right to *privacy* is a cornerstone in the Islamic legal system. The protection of such right is given precedent over the need of the community to punish the criminal. It is deemed more appropriate for Islamic legislation that "crimes" committed in private, and which result in no public harm or disturbance, should remain unnoticed by the authorities. Investigating such crimes would risk invading the private domain of the family and the individual. This means that crimes in Islam fall into two main categories: those which can be prosecuted without major invasion of privacy, and those which can not be pursued without interference in the private lives of the people. Only the first category should be prosecuted. But even within that category many crimes have gone unpunished. Islamic law urges those who commit any crime in private to keep it secret. Thus the Prophet urged "those of you who commit a filthy deed should keep it secret, his secret will be kept by God. But if he declares his deed, he is subject to punishment." The Prophet stated, "The farthest from God on the day of judgement are the announcers," and when asked who the "announcers" were, said, "it is the person who commits a shameful deed during the night where God provided him with secrecy, but in the morning he announces that he committed such and such acts."[17]

Islamic law also discourages the reporting of crimes by an uninvolved party by requiring that whoever accuses another of a crime should provide conclusive evidence of the latter's guilt. Failure to provide such proof may subject the accuser to severe punishment, sometimes as harsh as has been mentioned in the accusation of adultery.

If on the other hand, despite the above discouragement, the offender confesses or makes his deed public, the authorities have no choice but to prosecute him. In the case of the Saudi princess executed for adultery in the film mentioned earlier, it was generally agreed that, had she kept her affair a secret, nothing would have happened to her or her partner. Instead her insistence on publicizing the relationship forced her punishment.

Protection of privacy is not the only consideration in discouraging the publicizing of crimes. The need to avoid bad examples is another aim of Islamic law. A high frequency of crimes, even if severely punished, lessens public disapproval toward crime and encourages others to violate the law.

Islam placed great emphasis on setting good example and the display of public morality as a major deterrent to criminal acts. Publicity given to crimes is detrimental to this aim. For a high frequency of crimes tends to lessen the reluctance of individuals to follow the example of the criminal elements. The public gets used to crime if they continue to hear news of criminal acts. The psychological impact of crime is lost and the public indignation that works as preventive measure is weakened. Publicizing the crime is in itself a crime . . . and a publicly committed crime should be considered as two crimes. A person is both legally and morally wrong if he spreads the news of a crime . . . for he is in effect encouraging people to commit them.[18]

In addition to setting a bad example, frequent news of crimes, even if punished, undermines the authority of the leaders by creating the impression of lawlessness; and the news contributes to a general state of fear and disorder. For this reason some jurists believe that any publicized crime is in fact two crimes! Both may or may not be carried out by the same individual. These jurists find support for their views in Quranic statements such as the one instructing the believers to ". . . avoid suspicion for some of it is always untrue. Do not spy on each other and do not speak disparagingly of others in their absence."[19]

Under the concept of spying goes much of what modern criminal laws call investigation. Islamic jurists draw a distinction between investigation aimed at finding out whether a crime has been committed, investigation when some evidence (not conclusive) indicates that a crime has been committed, and investigation when clear evidence (e.g., a body) indicates a crime. The former is discouraged as presenting a danger to the right of privacy. On the other hand, if the crime is a matter of public record, as in the case of finding a dead body in the street, but the offender is not known, then the duty of the authorities in this case is to pursue the investigation until the offender is apprehended. Not to take action in this case would weaken the respect for the government and would create the public fear that is worse than the possibility of invasion of privacy. In this latter case it is the duty of the authority to establish a balance between the two important rights, that of the victim and that of citizens' privacy. Restriction of the process of investigation has made confession the most important basis for conviction in criminal law in Islam. Confession did not always work, however. Some are known to have confessed to crimes they did not commit simply because the appearances were so incriminating that they thought no one would believe their innocence. During the rule of Ali, there is a record of a case in which a man was found near a water well, kneeling over a dead man's body, holding a knife stained with blood. He was arrested and brought to trial; he confessed to killing the man and was sentenced to death. Before the sentence was carried out, another man came to Ali and confessed to the crime. When requestioned, the first man admitted that he had never killed the man, that he had killed a cow and was on his way to the well to wash the knife when he found the dead man. While he bent over to find out what was wrong with him, other people arrived and saw him. Realizing that the appearances were overwhelmingly against him, he decided to confess and to settle his account later with God.[20]

The idea of appearance is another point that separates Islamic criminal justice from other systems. The emphasis on privacy and the restriction on investigation are extended to include exploring the state of mind of the offender. This gives a different meaning to the concept of criminal causation and in particular to the concept of criminal intent.

It is not enough in modern legal systems to establish a material link between the activities of the offender and the criminal results. In the case of homicide, for example, it is not sufficient to prove that the death of the victim is related to the acts of the offender. The latter must have "intended" to cause such result. "Intent" in modern criminal laws is a complex idea involving two distinct aspects. It implies first a sound mind, more frequently defined as the ability to distinguish between right and wrong; that is, there must be the capacity to realize the nature of the act committed. The second aspect is free will, or the capacity to chose to commit or not to commit the act. Both are the essence of the ethical foundation underlying allocation of responsibility in modern criminal codes. The first of these aspects exempts from legal responsibility insane individuals, nonhuman animals, objects, and even children beyond the legal age, which varies in the different legal systems. The degree of choice, on the other hand, varies, and along with it varies the degree of culpability for the crime. Where the perpetrator is given no choice, as with physical coercion, he is assumed not to be responsible, even though he knows his act constitutes a crime. This is the basis for self-defense or justifiable homicide. Other less coercive influences, while they do not negate the choice completely, may reduce one's ability to restrain himself from committing the crime nonetheless. It is in this area that we distinguish between first- and second-degree murder and manslaughter.

Islamic law, while recognizing the importance of the moral and ethical responsibility of the offender, does not neglect the feelings of the victims and their kin groups either. As in the case of modern law, insanity also negates resonsibility in Islamic law. Thus an insane person who commits murder cannot be killed for his crime.

This however, does not negate the right of the victim's relatives to obtain compensation from the offender and his family.

Islamic law differs from modern laws in the way it assesses intent. Despite references to "intentional" and "nonintentional" deaths, Islamic law does not attempt to establish it by probing the state of mind of the offender. Intent rather, is *assumed* on the basis of physical evidence associated with the way the crime was commited, in particular the type of weapon used. An "intentional" death is that caused by a lethal weapon regardless of what the offender had in mind when committing the crime. The assumption is that one who is serious about killing another is likely to use a weapon that is capable of producing the result effectively. To justify this point, jurists maintain that such a method serves the interest of the community and those of the parties involved by insuring a speedy and just trial. According to this view, relying on visible evidence eliminates arguing about what was in the mind of the offender at the time, something that no one can prove for sure.

While Islamic law favors the victims in the assessment of criminal responsibility, it does not deprive the offender of certain considerations. While it assumes that the ideal state in the Islamic community is that of justice, it also recognizes that such an ideal state is far from being a reality. For this reason, it takes into consideration the circumstances and motivation in such crimes; a theft by a hungry man who steals to feed himself or his family is not liable to punishment.

Islamic Law and The Family

Despite the individualistic emphasis underlying the concept of umma, the rights and privileges given to the kinship groupings in pre-Islamic Arabia found strong expression in Islamic law. The major difference, however, is that instead of the large groups, such as the tribes and clans of the earlier period, Islam places the family as the center of its social order. The family becomes the building block of the umma. It is the "factory" that produces new Muslims, and it is the training agency through which the basic Islamic values and teachings are transmitted. Moreover, Islam looks upon the family as the most important mechanism for regulating the powerful and potentially disruptive force of sexual desire. Built on the basis of free and voluntary contractual relationship between a man and a woman, the family becomes the symbol of individual freedom on the one hand and the basis of societal integration on the other. Deeming the family too vital an institution to be left to the good will of individuals, Islam has provided extensive regulation for family relations. Detailed specification of the rights and duties of its members, and the processes by which it is formed, have been provided by Islamic law.

> Because of the novelty of the family structure in Muhammad's revolutionary social order, he had to modify in detail its regulations. Sex is one of the insticts whose satisfaction was regulated at length by the religious law during the first years of Islam.[21]

Not only did Islam organize interfamily relations, but it also provided a guideline for relating the family to other families. It is worth noting here that Islam did not relate the family to other families on a genealogical but on a territorial basis. Relationship between a family and its neighbors became important. Thus the regulation of the concept of *jiwar* or neighborliness. One might argue that this might be an indirect acknowledgement of the genealogical ties, since in a kinship-based society, neighbors are likely to be also close relatives. But the fact that Islam emphasized neighborliness and not kinship ties reflects the attempt to undermine the importance of the large kinship groups that dominated the social and political life of pre-Islamic society.

In the process of strenghtening the family, however, Islam has bestowed upon it many of the rights and privileges that the larger kinship units had in the earlier times.

One of these privileges was a measure of autonomy, but the family autonomy was established in its relationship to the larger kinship units and not vis-a-vis the state. This latter has subjected the family to close legal scrutiny and interfered in even the most intimate aspects of family relations. While these regulations applied to both male and female members of the family, those pertaining to women have attracted more attention both within and outside the Muslim world. Some of the most persistent stereotypes about Islam in the West stem from what is perceived as the treatment of Muslim women. Practices such as polygyny, seclusion, and the veil have become easy symbols for the Western media to use in their portrayal of Islamic society as backward and out of touch with modern reality.

On the other hand, these very practices have recently been used as symbols of the rejection of Western ideology by some groups within

Muslim societies. These groups attempt to emphasize the immoral aspects of Western societies as manifested in women's lack of modesty and in their rejection of their roles as women. Not only men but also women in such countries as Iran and Egypt have in recent years looked upon the veil as a symbol of national liberation, just as it was in Algeria's struggle for independence. Watching the events in Iran, especially the *chador*-clad women demonstrating in support of the Ayatollah Khomeini, students have frequently asked me how women could support someone who wants them to wear veils to the U.N. Women's Conference in Copenhagen. A *Time* magazine observer noted with puzzlement (and disapproval) that "Iranian delegates took two hours at the press conference to denounce the U.S. and to sing the joys of Islamic body covering . . . ," and watched with surprise as delegate Akram Hariri "managed to transform the chador into a symbol of liberation."[22] What *Time* and the majority of the Western media do not realize is that the chador *is* a symbol of liberation, that the idea of "liberation" has different meanings in different societies, and that Muslim and third-world women set different priorities and goals for their movements. Women in many Muslim countries today feel that their liberation as women is closely linked to the liberation of their societies from foreign influence, and that their immediate goal is to be part of a national mobilization that includes both men and women.

The veil, of course, has never been proved to be of Islamic origin, although female modesty is stressed in Islam.

It would be a mistake, however, to assume that women in these societies are sacrificing their own interest for the national cause, or as the *Time* article described, that they "slavishly follow the dictate of their male-dominated foreign offices." Nor is the trend restricted to the educated, ideologically committed women in these societies. Many women without any political involvement genuinely feel that their best interest is served under the traditional Islamic system and that the process of modernization—rather than giving them any advantage—is adding to the their burden.

This is not to say that within these societies no efforts are made to initiate social, political, and legal reforms which would benefit women. Such efforts have existed in many of the Muslim countries, and they are supported by both men and women.

The results have been significant gains for women in such fields as education, politics, and employment. Legal reforms, and in particular those related to personal status and family law, have had mixed results in the Muslim world. One reason is the lack of agreement on the meaning of reform. To some, it means replacing the Islamic-based family law with secular, Western-inspired ones. These views are held by those who believe that Islamic law assumes that women are inferior beings. The main support for their conclusion is the famous verse in Sura *al-Nisa* which states that:

> . . . men are guardians over women for God has preferred the one over the other and because men spend of their money. The good wives are those who are obedient and keep in their husband's absence what God would have them guard. Those whom you fear are disobedient, advise; if this does not work, desert their beds, then beat them lightly. If they submit to you, however, do not seek a way against them. . . .[23]

Others do not see a need for major legal changes, on the assumption that Islamic law is suitable for all times and places, and that it provides more protection and respect for women than the secular laws of many Western countries. They maintain that Islamic law is flexible enough to accommodate any changes deemed necessary. Inequality of women, according to those views, is a matter of interpretation and not of rigid rules in Islamic law. The flexibility of Islamic law has been demonstrated by the personal status and family laws in Tunisia. While retaining the essence of Islamic law, Tunisian legislators took advantage of the varying interpretation of these laws by Islamic jurists and by careful selection were able to come up with an Islamic-based law that is almost indistinguishable from any Western law.

Let us examine briefly some aspects of the laws of marriage and divorce in Islam. According to Islamic law, marriage is a civil contract between a man and a woman which starts with the request by one party and the acceptance by the other. Marriage may be contracted only between a man and a woman who are both of age and both of sound mind. If they are related by kinship, this relationship should be of a degree that is not prohibited by law. Mentally incompetent individuals and those who are under age (legal age varies from country to country) can be married only by permission of their guardians. The presence of two credible witnesses is a prerequisite for the validity of the contract. Islam considers the marriage contract among the "agreement" contracts (*'uqud al taradi*) and not a "formal" contract (*'aqd shakli*). As such, no writing or registration are required for its validation. Some countries still recognize the voluntary and informal nature of the contract. This form is prevalent in rural and predominantly tribal areas in the Middle East where the level of literacy is very low. Most of the Muslim countries, while recognizing the legal and spiritual validity of unwritten contracts, and while considering such contracts valid for paternity purposes, make it difficult to carry out other *legal implications* of the marriage contract such as inheritance and alimony without a registered document. Thus the Tunisian law states that the agreement of the parties, even if witnessed, cannot be accepted as a valid legal document unless carried out by an official authorized to carry out such a contract and witnessed in the legally prescribed manner.

While the Tunisian legislature cites the need to eliminate disagreement among the parties as the basis for requiring the registration of the marriage contract, the main purpose for each requirement is to prevent circumventing the rules prohibiting polygyny.

For the marriage contract to become effective, a certain amount of money (*mahr*) is to be paid by the groom to the bride. Part of the mahr is due at the signing of the marriage contract. This part is called the *muqaddam*, or the advance. The rest of the mahr becomes due upon the death of the husband or in the case of divorce. The amount of the mahr, as well as the proportion of the muqaddam to the *muakhar,* or dowry, vary from case to case, depending on the bargaining power of the two parties and/or their representatives. However, Islamic law requires that the mahr should be suitable for the woman, taking into consideration the social position of her family. The mahr is not a price for the wife, as it is sometimes referred to in Western literature, but a compulsory gift which becomes the private property of the wife. Part of the money is usually used for outfitting the bride and to help furnish the house.

The marriage contract gives the couple involved a number of rights vis-a-vis each other. The first and most important of these rights is that of sexual access. While the husband has an exclusive right to his wife's sexual activities, the wife's right on the other hand is limited by polygyny which is permitted by Islamic law. The basis of polygyny is the verse in Sura *al-Nisa* which states:

". . . marry of the women whom you please, two, three or four. But if you fear you cannot be just (to all of them) then only one."[24]

Polygyny is probably the most controversial aspect of family law in Islam. It has been singled out by antagonists of Islamic law as the symbol of women's degradation, and as the basis for calling for a secular law that better meets the realities of modern life. Abolishing, or at least limiting, polygyny has been the main target for reformists and feminist movements in the Muslim countries. Some have found grounds for such restriction in the same Quranic sura that permits polygny. They argue that since being just to all wives is impossible, there are simply no conditions under which the license could be exercised. But those who hold such views are in the minority. Most Islamic jurists today maintain that polygyny is an undisputed right in Islamic law, and that it is essential that it be retained even if monogamy is stated as a condition in a given marriage contract.

Although Islam does not provide justification for the practice of polygyny, jurists do. To them, polygyny fulfills an essential social function because it helps stem immorality by providing the married man the opportunity to marry the woman he desires instead of having her as a mistress. They further argue that it enables a man whose wife is sick, or unable to fulfill her marital obligations for no fault of her own, to continue to support her while having a normal and legitimate marital relationship with another woman.

Despite strong support for polygyny among Islamic jurists, pressure to place limitations on that right has been intensifying in some Muslim countries in recent years. In some cases such pressure has succeeded in changing the law. The most successful efforts have been in Tunisia where polygyny is outlawed. The Tunisian legislature has justified its bold move to prohibit polygyny by reference to the idea of "public interest" as the overriding principle in Islamic law. Their point is that Islam *allowed* (not condoned) polygyny for special circumstances that were peculiar to the social and political conditions during the early years of Islam. Among these was the need to accommodate some of the practices that had a strong following at the time, and thus to avoid direct confrontation over such practices when Islam was still in its formative stage. Since polygyny was widely practiced (with no limits on the number of wives) in pre-Islamic Arabia, Islam continued the practice (with limitations to four wives) for the time being. Another consideration was the existence of a state of war in the early years of Islam which took the lives of many men, leaving large numbers of women without men to support them. Such conditions, which had justified the legalization of polygyny in the early years of Islam, are no longer present in today's Tunisia. On the contrary, polygyny runs counter to the social policies of the country, especially those relating to economic development. Polygyny has therefore become contrary to the public interest.[25]

Tunisian law is unique among contemporary Islamic legislations in its clear and unconditional banning of polygyny. Legislations in some of the other Muslim countries have succeeded only in limiting the right. Moroccan law allows polygyny but prohibits it in specific cases where there is a strong indication that it would place undue hardship on the first wife. It further requires that the new wife be informed of the previous marriage(s) as a condition for the validation of her marriage.

Iraqi law also requires a court permission for the man to have an additional wife. Such permission is not granted by the court unless the man demonstrates his ability to support more than one wife, and unless he provides convincing reasons for his desire to have an additional wife. Violation of these conditions subjects the man to a prison term of no more than one year.

Despite the efforts of many groups in Egypt to limit polygyny since the turn of the century, the Egyptian legislature has so far failed to put a serious curb on the legality of polygyny. After fifteen years of debate, the new personal status and family law approved in May, 1980 offers very little in terms of major revisions. With regard to polygyny the only condition introduced is that the first wife should be informed of the impending marriage and is, if she chooses, given the right to get a divorce. Considering the rules regarding alimony for divorced wives (which entitle them to no more than one year's support alimony), few women would consider this provision to be a real option.

It is important to note here that polygyny is a legal problem and not a social one. Social and practical considerations have limited the actual practice of polygyny to an extremely small fraction of the population of the Muslim world. The legality of polygyny in most of these countries has symbolic significance in women's struggle to adjust their roles and images to the challenges of their changing societies.

The second of the marriage rights is that of obedience, or *habs*; it belongs only to the husband. The word "habs" means "detention," and it implies the right of the man to keep the woman in the marital house. The right of habs has its basis in a paragraph in the Quran which reads: "They [women] should not go out of the house lest they commit a grave sin." The wife may leave the marital house without the permission of the husband only to visit her immediate relatives, especially her parents. (She may visit her parents once a week without the husband's permission.) Relatives other than the parents are not covered under the license, and she is entitled to visit them only once a year without the permission of the husband. These visits do not include staying overnight, however. If such a stay is planned, even with her parents, she must obtain the husband's permission.

Habs entitles a man to prevent his wife from going outside the house, for example, to work or attend school. According to the majority of Islamic jurists, when a woman goes out without the permission of her husband to work or to school, she undermines his right of habs. A woman who violates that right is defined as disobedient (or *nashis*) and, therefore, not entitled to financial support by the husband. On the other hand, some jurists restrict the husband's right to detain his wife to instances of direct conflict, as when a job would take her away from home for long periods of time. A move to redefine the right of habs so as to accommodate the growing need and demand for women's work has been underway in some Muslim countries. In Egypt, the committee formed in 1967 to draft the proposal for revised personal status and family law has dealt with the problems of working wives. The proposed article 85 of that draft states that: "A wife may go out of the house in the case of necessity and in cases permitted by custom. . . . Her going out to work is not considered a violation of the right of *habs* if she specifies going outside the house as a condition in the marriage contract."

The wording of this article makes it clear that the normal condition is one in which the woman stays in the house, and that work is the exception rather than the rule. The committee decided that a man must understand from the beginning that his marriage contract specifies the legal right of his wife to work. Only then can a marriage contract legally insure a wife the right to work or pursue an education without her husband's permission, since the husband will have had the opportunity to refuse to marry a woman making these contractual demands. Even when such a condition is included in the marriage contract, the husband, according to the new proposal, has the right to violate that condition and prevent his wife from working if her work "puts unnecessary hardship upon him." The definition of what constitutes an unnecessary hardship is left to the husband. Final revisions have failed to deal effectively with this point.

Another point of controversy in personal status and family law is the different access to divorce given to men and women. According to Islamic law, a man is allowed to dissolve a marriage merely by pronouncing the dismissal formula "I divorce you" in the presence of credible witnesses. The husband need have no grounds for the divorce. A husband who has divorced his wife can reverse the process merely by living with her again as a husband if he does this during the *idda*, the waiting period of three months following the divorce. No new contract is needed in this case.

The idda is a period during which the woman cannot marry another man. Its main purpose is to make sure that if the woman is carrying a child fathered by the husband, there will be no conflict regarding paternity. If the husband does not take back his wife during the idda period, he cannot thereafter do so without a new contract. The divorce in the latter case is called *bain,* or absolute, in contrast to the *ragi,* or temporary divorce during the idda period. If the husband exercises his right of absolute divorce three times, he cannot remarry his wife unless the latter is married first to another man, or *muhallal,* then divorced by him.

The woman does not have the same right of divorce as the man. She cannot divorce her husband except by establishing adequate grounds for divorce and obtaining a court decision. The grounds specified by Islamic law for divorce initiated by a woman are:

1) Inability or unwillingness of the husband to support his wife.
2) Incurable illness of the husband. This applies to mental as well as physical illness.
3) Social inconvenience, defined vaguely as any conditions created by the husband which put on the wife a heavy burden to which she is not accustomed.
4) The absence of the husband for more than a year without good reason.
5) The imprisonment of the husband for more than three years.

With the exception of the case of divorce on the basis of lack of financial support, the divorce by the court is always bain, or absolute. Whether the divorce is initiated by the husband or the wife, the wife is theoretically entitled to alimony for the period of idda. This is not always the case in practice, however. In many instances, the husband will make the wife forfeit her right to alimony as a condition of granting her the divorce. In certain cases, a wife or her parents may even pay the husband a sum of money to obtain the divorce, especially when the wife does not have adequate grounds, thus avoiding going to the court.

To justify this discrimination between men and women in the area of divorce, some Islamic jurists refer to differences in temperament between men and women. Women, by the very nature of their role as mothers, it is claimed, are more emotional and thus less capable of making rational decisions. Therefore, they argue, to base the stability of the family upon their impulsive decisions would be to undermine the whole institution of marriage. They also believe that giving a judge the right to make decisions regarding divorce (rather than leaving it in the hands of the husband) would expose family secrets to public examination. Besides, they maintain, though the right of the husband may appear unchecked, there are many social and practical considerations which impose severe restrictions on that right.

Advocates of women's rights reject this argument. First, they hold that there is no proof that one sex is inherently more (or less) emotional than the other. Second, if exposing the family secrets is the main reason for not requiring the husband to go to court for a divorce, why is it not a consideration in the case of the wife seeking a divorce, since in the latter case the family secrets are equally exposed?

As in the case of polygyny, moves to reform the rules of divorce have mixed results. The new revision of personal status and family law in Egypt has introduced very little in terms of changes in divorce procedures for both men and women. Divorce is still an absolute right for the man, to be exercised at will, and with little formal inter-ference from the legal institutions. The only requirement added by the new rules is that the wife should be notified of the action either by the husband or by the court. No steps have been taken even to speed up procedures whose slowness has been a major complaint of the women. As a result, the old system in which divorce sometimes takes ten years or more is still in effect. During such period the woman is in a state of limbo. She is not married and therefore not entitled to the right of support by the husband, nor is she free to seek other marital arrangements that might provide her with some sense of security. The procedures are even slower in the new laws because of the introduction of the reconciliation committees.

These are only a few aspects of personal status and family law in Islam. Since family law is the only part of Islamic law that is still applied in most of the Muslim countries, it has direct implication for the social and economic policies of these countries.

From the brief discussion of the above aspects, one gets the impression, and justifiably so, that these laws provide unequal treatment for men and women. Such discrimination can be detrimental to the national policies if such policies call for increased participation of women in the labor force and a higher degree of freedom of movement. The right of habs given to the husband can interfere in these policies. But to blame Islam for the retention of these rules is short-sighted. Islamic law in practically all its aspects is characterized by a great degree of flexibility that could be used to introduce many of the new ideas. The Tunisian legislature demonstrated that in the case of family laws. Rather, Islamic law should be viewed as a reflection and not the cause of some of the conservative views in Muslim societies, especially those relating to the attitudes towards women and their activities. The position of women in these societies is not solely the product of laws, even unjust ones, but of long traditions whose connection to Islam in general, and Islamic laws in particular, is not always clear. Legal reform may change the formal aspect of the inequality between men and women, but only changes in the attitude of Muslim society will ensure the actual equality of men and women. This does not imply that legal reform is useless, for it is important. It means simply that legal reform is not enough. In addition to its practical and symbolic value, legal reform might, in the long run, effect changes in attitudes by creating norms supportive of the new role of women. But until such changes in attitude are evident, no legal reform, however substantial, can result in a magical transformation of the traditional role of the Muslim woman into a modern one.

Notes

Part I
Islamic Revival or Reaffirmation

1. Cited in Lewis H. Lapham, "America's Foreign Policy: A Rake's Progress," *Harper's Magazine,* Vol. 258 (March 1979), p. 36.
2. Muhammad Asad, *The Principles of State and Government in Islam* (Berkeley and Los Angeles: University of California Press, 1961), p. 2.
3. Ibid., p. 3.
4. Gustave E. von Grunebaum, *Medieval Islam: A Study in Cultural Orientation* (Chicago: University of Chicago Press, 1962), p. 142.
5. Material in this section adapted from Don Peretz, *The Middle East Today,* 3rd ed. (New York: Holt, Rinehart & Winston, 1978), Ch. 2.
6. Fazlur Rahman, *Islam* (Garden City, N.Y.: Doubleday & Co., Anchor Books, 1968), p. 84.
7. Ibid., p. 87.
8. Von Grunebaum, op. cit., pp. 322 ff.
9. Asad, op. cit., p. 3.
10. Ibid., pp. 13-14.
11. Ibid., p. 3.
12. Ibid., p. 4.
13. Ibid., p. 5.
14. Ibid., pp. 5-6.
15. Ibid., p. 96.
16. Ibid., p. 21.
17. Ibid., p. 20.
18. Ibid., pp. 22-23.
19. Cited in Richard P. Mitchell, *The Society of Muslim Brothers* (London: Oxford University Press, 1969), p. 245.
20. Ibid.
21. Ibid., p. 246.
22. Asad, op. cit., p. 25.
23. Ibid., p. 26.
24. Ibid., p. 27.
25. Ibid., p. 28.
26. *Foreign Broadcast Information Service* (FBIS), Vol. V, No. 236 (December 6, 1979). Supplement 034 of the "Daily Report: Middle East and North Africa" contains an English translation of the Constitution of the Islamic Republic of Iran, p. 7.
27. Ibid., Principle 11, p. 15.
28. Asad, op. cit., p. 32.
29. Mitchell, op. cit., pp. 264-265.

30. FBIS, op. cit., Principle 56, p. 20.

31. Sheikh Ahmed (ed.), *Law and Constitution: Some Salient Features of the Islamic Law and Constitution* (Karachi: Pakistan Institute of Arts and Design, no date), Article 21, p. 57.

32. Asad, op. cit., p. 40.

33. Mitchell, op. cit., p. 246.

34. FBIS, op. cit., Principle 115, p. 28.

35. Ibid., Principle 5, p. 14.

36. Ibid., Principle 109, p. 27.

37. Ibid., Principle 110, p. 27.

38. Ibid., Principle 144, p. 31.

39. Asad, op. cit., pp. 40-41.

40. Mitchell, op. cit., pp. 246-247.

41. Asad, op. cit., p. 45.

42. Ibid., p. 46.

43. Sheikh Ahmed, op. cit., p. 42.

44. Mitchell, op. cit., p. 248.

45. FBIS, op. cit., Principle 13, p. 15.

46. Muaamar el-Qaddafi (Muammar Al Qathafi), *The Green Book, Part One. The Solution of the Problem of Democracy: The Authority of the People* (Tripoli: Public Establishment for Publishing, Advertising and Distribution, no date), p. 26.

47. Ibid., pp. 28-29.

48. Ibid., p. 32.

49. Sheikh Ahmed, op. cit., p. 74.

50. Ibid., p. 76.

51. FBIS, op. cit., p. 13.

52. Ibid., Principle 31, p. 17.

53. Sheikh Ahmed, op. cit., Article 43, p. 63.

54. Ibid., pp. 63-64.

55. Mitchell, op. cit., pp. 251-252.

56. Ibid., p. 253.

57. Muaamar el-Qaddafi (Muammar Al Qathafi), op. cit., *Part Two. The Solution of the Economic Problem: Socialism,* p. 15.

58. Ibid., pp. 18-19, 30.

59. Ibid., pp. 13-14.

60. Ibid., p. 32.

61. Ibid., pp. 29-30.

62. Mitchell, op. cit., p. 252.

63. Cited in Muhammad Imran, *An Outline of the Economic System of Islam* (Lahore: Islamic Book Centre, no date), p. 6.

64. Ibid., p. 16.

65. Asad, op. cit., p. 90.

66. Ibid., p. 41.

67. Ibid., p. 74.

68. F. Rahman, op. cit., pp. 35-36.

69. FBIS, op. cit., p. 8.

70. Ibid., Principle 21, p. 16.

71. Mitchell, op. cit., p. 255.

72. Ibid., p. 257.

73. Majid Khadduri, *War and Peace in the Law of Islam* (Baltimore: Johns Hopkins Press, 1955), p. 46.

74. Afzal Iqbal, *The Prophet's Diplomacy. The Art of Negotiations* as *Conceived and Developed by the Prophet of Islam* (Cape Cod, Mass.: Claude Stark, 1975), p. 10.

75. Khadduri, op. cit., pp. 47-48.

76. Ibid., p. 220.

77. Ibid., pp. 55-56.

78. Mitchell, op. cit., p. 226.

79. Ibid., pp. 226-227.

80. Ibid., pp. 230-231.

81. Asad, op. cit., p. 7.

82. Ibid., pp. 98-99.

83. *Al Ahram* (Cairo: June 14, 1979), p. 1.

Part II

Islam and Development

1. Max Weber, *The Protestant Ethic and the Spirit of Capitalism* (first published 1904).

2. Leonard Binder, *Religion and Politics in Pakistan* (Berkeley & Los Angeles: University of California Press, 1961).

3. Fazlur Rahman, *Islam* (Chicago: University of Chicago Press, 1969), pp. 219-224.

4. Hisham Sharabi, "Islam and Modernization in the Arab World," in Thompson and Reischauer, eds., *Modernization of the Arab World* (New York: Van Nostrand, 1966), pp. 26-36; Charles Issawi, "The Arab World's Heavy Legacy," ibid., pp. 13-25; Majid Khadduri, "From Religious to National Law," ibid., pp. 37-51.

5. F. Rahman, op. cit., p. 241.

6. Maxime Rodinson, *Islam and Capitalism,* trans. by Brian Pearce (New York: Pantheon, 1974), p. 99.

7. Rodinson, op. cit., pp. 30-32.

8. Roger Owen, "Islam and Capitalism: a Critique of Rodinson," *Review of Middle East Studies,* Vol. 2 (1976), p. 90.

9. Rodinson, op. cit., p. 208.

10. Rodinson, op. cit., p. 217.

11. S. Habashi, "Islam and Sharia in Foreign Trade," *Arab Economist,* No. 42 (London: December 1979), pp. 14-16 (in Arabic).

12. Ibid., p. 15.

13. Ibid., p. 16.

14. Bernard Lewis, "Communism and Islam," *International Affairs,* Vol. 30, pp. 1-12.

15. Kathleen R.G. Glavanis, "Cold War Ideology and Middle East History," Review of Middle East Studies, Vol. 2 (1976), pp. 35-43.

16. Malcolm Kerr, "Islam and Arab Socialism," *Muslim World,* Vol. 56 (1966), p. 277.

17. I. Wallerstein, *The Modern World System* (New York: Academic Press, 1974), pp. 348-350.

18. Gamal Abdel Nasser, quoted in *Arab Observer,* No. 169 (September 16, 1963), p. 19.

19. Sharabi, op. cit., p. 31.

20. George Masannat, "Nasser's Search for New Order," *Muslim World,* Vol. 56 (April, 1966), p. 93.

21. Nissim Rejwan, *Nasserist Ideology* (New Brunswick, N.J.: Transaction Books, 1974), p. 46.

22. Mohamad Hasanyn Haykal, *al-Ahram* (August 4, 1961), cited in Rejwan, op. cit., pp. 96-98.

23. Kerr, op. cit., p. 277.

24. Muhammad Awda, "On the Search for Theory" (in Arabic), *Rose al-Yusuf* (January 9, 1961), cited in Rejwan, op. cit., p. 75.

25. Mohammad Amin Rahman, "Religion is Not a War Against Progress" (in Arabic), Al Talia (Cairo: June 1976), p. 87.

26. David C. Gordon, "Algeria," *Muslim World,* Vol. 56 (1966), p. 285.

27. Jean Leca, "Algerian Socialism: Nationalism, Industrialization and State Building," in Desfosses and Levesque, eds., *Socialism in the Thrid World* (New York: Praeger, 1975), pp. 132-133.

28. Ibid., p. 132.

29. Ibid., p. 139.

30. Ibid., p. 135 f.

31. G.A. Heeger, "Socialism in Pakistan," in Desfosses and Levesque, op. cit., p. 295.

32. Ibid., p. 296.

33. Ibid., p. 298-305.

34. Sami A. Hanna, "Al-Afghani: A Pioneer of Islamic Socialism," *Muslim World,* Vol. 56 (1966), pp. 24-32.

35. S.A. Hanna & G.H. Gardner, "Islam Socialism," *Muslim World,* Vol. 56 (1966), pp. 71-86.

36. Ibid., p. 76.

37. Ibid., p. 79.

38. Ibid., p. 77.

39. Sharabi, op. cit.: The skepticism of the secularist remains unshaken. Thus, Rejwan writes "Islam . . . has in practice never been taken by the educated politically-conscious contemporary Muslim Arabs to entail the kind of socio-political ideology deemed necessary for the establishment and maintenance of a modern state. Thus we find that, while professing whole-hearted adherence to Islam and its premises, the overwhelming majority of present-day Muslim Arab thinkers and political activists continue to toy with the leading socio-political ideologies of the day, examining the merits and demerits of these . . . from the viewpoint of their suitability to their own situations." (Rejwan, op. cit., p. 32.)

40. Muhammad Abdul Rauf, *The Islamic Doctrine of Economics and Contemporary Economic Thought* (Washington, D.C.: American Enterprise Institute, 1978). p. 17.

41. al-Sadek al-Mahdi, "Islam and Social Transformation," *Arab Economist* (Cairo: March 1979).

42. Muaammar el-Qaddafi (Muammar Al Qathafi), *The Green Book: Part II. The Solution of the Economic Problem: Socialism* (Tripoli: Public Establishment for Publishing).

43. Mohammad Nejatullah Siddiqi, "Teaching Economics at the University Level in Muslim Countries," *Islam and the Modern Age,* Vol. 9 (February 1978), pp. 16-34.

44. Ibid., p. 18.

45. Ibid., p. 21.

46. To name but a few names, Abdallah Laroui of Morocco, Mahfud Benoune of Algeria, Samir Amin, Mohammad Anis and Mohammad Dowidar of Egypt.

47. A.A.K. Soze, "Marxism and Islam," *Islam and the Modern Age,* Vol. 10, No. 2 (May 1979), p. 61.

Part III
Islam: The Legal Dimension*

1. W. Montgomery Watt, *Islam and the Integration of Society* (London: Rutledge & Keegan Paul, 1961), p. 7.

2. H.A.R. Gibb, "Constitutional Organization," in M. Khaduri & H.J. Liebesny, eds., *Origin and Development of Islamic Law,* Vol. I (Washington, D.C.: Middle East Institute, 1955), p. 3.

3. Muhammad Abu-Zahra, *Falsafat al-'uquba fi el-fiqh al-Islami* (Cairo: Ma'had al Dirasat al-Arabiyya al-aliya, 1963), p. 43.

4. Ibid., p. 94.

5. Quran, Sura 16:67.

6. Quran, Sura 2:219.

7. Quran, Sura 4:43.

8. Shams al-Din al Sarakhsi, *Al-Mabsut* (no date), Part 24, p. 30.

9. Quran, Sura 5:93.

10. Abu-Bakr al-Kasani, *Bad'ai al-San'ai* (Cairo: 1328/1910), Part 5, p. 116.

11. Ibid., p. 117.

12. Abu-Zahra, op. cit., p. 96.

13. Quran, Sura 5:36.

14. Abu-Zahra, op. cit., p. 153.

15. Quran, Sura 24:2.

16. Binghamton *Evening Press* (September 6, 1980).

17. Abu-Zahra, op. cit., p. 31.

18. Ibid., p. 32.

19. Quran, Sura 49:12.

20. Ibn Qayyim al-Jawziyya, *Al-Turuq el Hikmiyya* (A.H. 1317/1899-1900), pp. 55-56.

21. Fatima Mernissi, *Beyond the Veil: Male-Female Dynamics in a Modern Muslim Society* (New York: Schenkman, 1975), p. xv.

22. *Time* Magazine (New York: August 4, 1980).

23. Quran, Sura 4:34.

24. Quran, Sura 4:3.

25. Mahammed Mansour, "Ahkam al-Zawaj al-mustahdatha bittashri' el-Tunisi," *The National Review of Social Sciences,* Vol. II (Tunis: 1974), p. 238.

*I wish to acknowledge with gratitude the editorial assistance of Professor Abkar Muhammad, Chairman, Afro-American and African Studies, S.U.N.Y., Binghamton.